JEFF BELANGER

The World's Most Haunted Places

Places

FROM THE SECRET FILES OF GHOSTVILLAGE.COM

New Page Books
A division of The Career Press, Inc.
Franklin Lakes, NJ

THE WORLD'S MOST HAUNTED PLACES
EDITED AND TYPESET BY CLAYTON W. LEADBETTER
Cover illustration and design by Jean William Naumann
Printed in the U.S.A. by Book-mart Press

To order this title, please call toll-free 1-800-CAREER-1 (NJ and Canada: 201-848-0310) to order using VISA or MasterCard, or for further information on books from Career Press.

The Career Press, Inc., 3 Tice Road, PO Box 687,
Franklin Lakes, NJ 07417
www.careerpress.com
www.newpagebooks.com

Library of Congress Cataloging-in-Publication Data

Belanger, Jeff.
   The world's most haunted places : from the secret files of ghostvillage.com / by Jeff Belanger.
      p. cm.
   Includes bibliographical references and index.
   ISBN 1-56414-764-9 (pbk.)
      1. Haunted places. 2. Ghosts. I. Title.

BF1461.B387 2004
133.1—dc22

2004048623

For Megan, whose love is supernatural.

Acknowledgments

There are many people who put forth a lot of effort to make this book happen. I'd like to thank my incredible wife, Megan, for her support, her critical eye, and her faith in me. Thank you to my entire family for relaying every ghost story they've ever heard. I'd like to thank my friends and colleagues who provided me with a sounding board when I needed it, feedback when appropriate, ideas all of the time, and a lot of support throughout the creation of this book: Lee Prosser, Jim DeCaro, Sean Snyderman, Gary Folz, Jerry Beach, Darci Faiello, Brent Richardson, Andy Laird, and Roberto Aberasturia just to name a few!

I'd also like to thank some giants I look up to: Jeffrey Wands, Troy Taylor, and Tamara Thorne.

In gathering supernatural accounts for this book, I interviewed scores of people around the world who shared their very personal experiences with me. I'd like to thank these brave souls for their contributions and trust. Without these great people, this book would not have been possible.

I'd also like to thank the folks at New Page Books, specifically Michael Pye, Clayton Leadbetter, Laurie Kelly, and Kirsten Beucler.

Last, but definitely not least, I would also like to thank the Ghostvillagers—a global community of people who not only care deeply about the study of ghosts and the supernatural, but who also care a lot about each other. Thank you all for touching my life in your own unique way.

Contents

Introduction

Ghostly legends and personal encounters with the supernatural get right down to the big question we all have: *Is there life after death?* That's the heart of the matter, really. When someone sees what they know to be the spirit of someone deceased, the big question is answered for that individual.

Around the world, there are buildings, cemeteries, and other man-made structures that have witnessed more history than any living person. Oh, if their walls could talk...but, sometimes they can. And do.

Oral traditions are mostly dead in our modern world. The ability to record events in writing, photographic form, and even video is accessible to everyone. But ghost stories are one of the very few exceptions to the rule. Millions of people have an unexplained brush with the supernatural every year. Some of the encounters are frightening, some touching, all are profound. Many people never document the time, place, weather conditions, exact GPS (Global Positioning System) location of the ghost, or anything else the scientific community would appreciate knowing. Why? My God, they just saw a ghost! The event is burned into the witness's permanent memory, and their brains and hearts are trying to figure out what just happened.

Maybe a few hours, days, or years down the road, the witness of the phenomenon may feel comfortable enough to share a very personal and intimate experience with someone they really trust.

Some ghost legends are centuries old, where people living local to the disembodied soul believe they know who the ghost was in life, and some might even speculate what unfinished business keeps the spirit earthbound. To study these spirits is to study history. The spirit world and our past are intertwined—there's a lot we can learn by studying both. Of course, some ghost stories only go back a few decades; they seem to have been born or stirred up by some event.

One of the first haunted places I ever researched was a 250-year-old restaurant near my home in Massachusetts. The owner started telling me about some of her peculiar experiences, and then she left me with the bartender, who had only worked there for a year and a half, and he started telling me of strange accounts that happened just a few months prior to my visit. A busboy walked by and asked if we were talking about the ghosts; he went on to give his own story from the few weeks prior. After I published the story on Ghostvillage.com, I received e-mails from people who also had supernatural experiences at this restaurant.

After this early research, I understood what it means for a place to be haunted. The phenomena must be repeatable and experienced by a wide array of people. True, we do hear about some of these encounters secondhand—that's oral tradition at work. As the secondhand stories spread to thirdhand and beyond, the experiences may become exaggerated into something Hollywood would cook up. But sometimes we get to hear these accounts right from the original witnesses.

Many ghost encounters tend to be subtle, but intense. Imagine being alone in a big, old, creaking house. It's a dark and stormy night, and as you reach for a doorknob and start to turn it, you feel an obvious force turn the knob against you, maybe a shuffling on the other side of the door. The room around you becomes suddenly chilled. Quickly turning the knob again and jerking the door open, you find that no one (well, no one that you can see anyway) is standing there.

Subtle, yes—and completely unnerving. Of course, the ghosts aren't always subtle. Sometimes they appear in front of people. Sometimes they even have something to say. It's important that we listen to the witnesses, to the ghosts, and to the history.

The World's Most Haunted Places is a world tour of historic locations and ghostly experiences. We'll traverse the globe and find some common threads to ghostly legends, some figures from history who have insisted on being remembered to the point where they are still seen and recognized for who they are or were. We'll listen to witnesses from many different walks of life tell us what they felt, heard, saw, and sometimes even smelled.

I'll be your tour guide for this global voyage into the supernatural. Please be respectful, as we will be visiting some hallowed grounds, homes where you'll be a guest, and other historically important locales where the walls, the grounds, and the ghosts *do* talk.

Chapter 1:
BALLYGALLY CASTLE HOTEL

Ballygally Castle, in County Antrim, is one of Northern Ireland's most haunted locations. Today it is a three-star hotel, and though no formal ghost tours are offered, the infamous "Ghost Room" is always open to guests who are brave enough to visit. Photo courtesy of Hastings Hotels.

BALLYGALLY CASTLE HOTEL:

Ballygally, Ireland

Tel: 44 (0) 28-2858-1066

Web: *www.hastingshotels.com/hotel_ballygally.html*

On a bright sunny day, Ballygally Castle is a living postcard—a charming, almost teal-colored Scottish baronial castle overlooking the sea in Northern Ireland. On a dark, stormy evening, Ballygally is right out of a 1950s horror movie. There's a dark coastal road that takes you to the castle on the hill. You can imagine the lightning flashes making Ballygally's Scottish granite flash a pale grey before going back to almost black in the night.

In a corner turret of the castle, a small window overlooks the North Channel of the Irish Sea from a small, drafty room the Ballygally staff have dubbed the "Ghost Room." No one stays in the Ghost Room overnight anymore—well, no one living anyway.

Today, Ballygally Castle is attached to a popular three-star hotel. From the outside, visitors can clearly see where the castle ends and the hotel was added on in the 1950s. Located about 20 miles north of Belfast, Ballygally was originally built by James Shaw, a Greenock, Scotland native who came to Northern Ireland in 1613. Shaw built the castle in 1625 in a French chateau style, with 5-foot-thick walls, a steep roof, and corner turrets. An open stream ran through the outer hall for convenient drinking water—plus the water meant the castle's occupants could hold out a long time if there was a siege.

Shortly after the completion of the castle's construction, James Shaw took a wife named Lady Isobel Shaw. The current legend says

15

that during the first few years of their marriage, Lady Shaw had a daughter. James Shaw became angry that his wife didn't produce a male heir, and so he locked her in the tiny turret of the castle facing the sea. It's unclear whether Lady Shaw leapt to her death from the small window while desperately trying to get to her daughter, or whether James Shaw had some henchmen throw her down the steep staircase, killing her.

The first time I heard this bit of folklore, it didn't sit right with me. If James Shaw was so upset about not getting a male heir, wouldn't the couple just try for another child? After some digging, I heard another version of the legend that seemed to make more sense. Apparently, Lady Shaw may have been having an affair with a seaman. One could also speculate that her daughter may have been the love child of this mysterious man. When James Shaw found out, he went into a rage, locking his wife in the turret. His rage built until it either drove Lady Shaw out the window, or some thugs threw her to her death.

Lady Shaw has been experienced in the old part of the castle and especially in the Ghost Room many times over the centuries. But Lady Shaw is certainly not the only ghost haunting Ballygally.

Olga Henry is the current manager of Ballygally Castle Hotel. Henry has worked at Ballygally since January of 2003, and though she's originally from Northern Ireland, she didn't hear about the ghost stories until she arrived at the castle for work. She was quickly indoctrinated about the ghosts at Ballygally. Henry said, "I'm sort of very skeptical about the whole supernatural thing and ghosts. But the more I stay here and work here, the more I think there's definitely something in this hotel."

In the old part of the hotel—the castle section—there are four guest rooms for rent situated below the Ghost Room. Some people specifically request the rooms in the castle section, and some get more of an experience than they bargained for. Henry told me about one of their guests who was staying in the old section of the castle while in town for business. She explained, "He was staying in one of the rooms in the tower, and he has little kids at home. In the middle of the night, he thought he was in his own house at home—he was lying face down in the bed and he thought one of his children had put their hand on his back. And then he woke up and sort of realized where he was, and he said that he could hear a child running about the room and laughing.

He then appeared at our reception area in just his boxer shorts, and he said, 'Just get me out of that old part of the castle!'"

The castle section is also home to two private dining rooms, one called the Dungeon Room and the other the 1625 Room. The Dungeon Room features an old-world stone floor, a grand fireplace, and rough-cast walls. It was in the Dungeon Room that Henry had quite a peculiar experience in December 2003.

Henry explained how a group of directors were coming to stay at the hotel and were going to dine the evening of their arrival in the Dungeon Room. She said, "We'd set the room up the day before. I made sure the glasses were sparkling, and the candelabra's right, and it all looks the part. After setting up, we had locked the room. The next day, these guys were checking in that morning, and I thought I'd go and open the Dungeon in case they wanted to have a look as to where they'd be dining. I went down and opened the Dungeon, and the table was an absolute mess.

"Nothing else in the room had been disturbed, but all the glasses on the table were laid in a circle around the table. The linen napkins had all been unfolded and sort of strewn across the table. We had a round mirror in the center of the table with the candelabra on it, and everything was covered—including the glasses—in a scum or a dust. It wasn't the dust that you just wipe off, it was like a scum. But no-where else in the room—it wasn't on the floor, it wasn't on any other surface in the room—just purely over the table. It definitely sent the hairs on the back of my neck up, because I'm thinking I had the key to this room, is there another key somewhere? And even so, I just couldn't explain how that happened. None of it made sense at all. It was very unnerving."

Though the older castle section of the hotel is the most active, ghosts have been experienced throughout the entire hotel. Henry told me about mediums who have come to Ballygally and said they may have more ghosts than guests on some evenings. Some common reports include the sounds of children laughing and running around playing, the rustling of a silk dress when no one is around to make such a sound, showers that turn themselves on and flood the rooms below, and there are many reports of ghostly knocks on guest room doors throughout the hotel. Whether that prank is ghostly, or very much earthly, guests report opening their doors to find no one in the hallway outside.

Lady Isobel Shaw's ghost does seem to be more confined to the castle section—especially the Ghost Room. The week before Halloween 1998, Kim Lenaghan, a reporter for the BBC radio program *Good Morning Ulster*, was recording a series of fun Halloween segments for the morning radio show and decided to spend the night in Ballygally Castle's Ghost Room as one of her segments. I spoke to Lenaghan from her office at the BBC in Belfast about that night at Ballygally, when she got a much bigger ghost story than she planned on. Lenaghan said, "We thought it would be a laugh. We thought: Let's go do the usual 'spend a night in the spooky house' story."

Lenaghan drove to Ballygally on a dark, stormy, and cold October evening. She had arranged to meet a psychic medium there, who would only go by the name of Sally. Sally didn't want publicity out of the news story; she was simply there to try to make contact. Like other mediums, Sally noted to the hotel management that there were several spirits haunting the hotel. Lenaghan and Sally made their way up to the cold and drafty Ghost Room, and Sally began to go through a meditation ritual to try to make contact with one of the spirits of Ballygally Castle. The Ghost Room is a tiny space with a wrought-iron cot bed, a basic dressing table with a small mirror on it, a chair, a few old pictures on the wall, and a small window that juts out to offer a view of the sea.

Lenaghan said Sally seemed to be making contact, and that's when the environment started to change. She said, "She was not in a trance, but she was certainly very focused on what she was doing. And I'm standing there with a tape recorder hoping for the best. The next thing that happened is it started to get a lot warmer. I mean significantly warmer—the temperature in the room must've gone up by 10 degrees. Then she [Sally] started talking to someone, literally coinciding with the temperature going up, and a smell came. It didn't waft in—I mean the smell came straight on almost instantly. It smelled like vanilla, but it wasn't exactly vanilla. While it was a vanilla-like smell, it was an old, slightly musty smell. Musty vanilla—I know it sounds ridiculous. But that's what it was."

At that point, the hairs on the back of Lenaghan's neck were up. The medium was having a conversation with someone in the room who was obviously distressed. Lenaghan likened the experience to listening to one side of a phone conversation. Sally was trying to calm down what she later called a very upset female spirit.

The medium would later explain that the spirit was that of a young woman who was scared and looking for her young daughter. The medium told Lenaghan that "they were keeping her there against her will, and she said there was an older woman who wouldn't let her out of the room." During the conversation, this woman continually ran to the window looking for a man named Robert who was out at sea. The spirit didn't understand why Robert didn't come back to get her.

The experience lasted 7 or 8 minutes before Sally's face went blank and she announced "I've lost her." Lenaghan said, "And I knew instantly because, as she said that, the smell disappeared. A normal smell cannot just come and go like that, it literally disappeared—there was no trace of it. Also, as it went, the temperature in the room started to drop dramatically."

Back downstairs, the medium told Lenaghan, who was to be spending the rest of the night alone in the Ghost Room, not to worry—that the spirit was not evil, just scared. Sally said she wasn't sure if the ghost would come back that night or not. Lenaghan was having her doubts about spending the night in the Ghost Room.

After midnight, the medium left and Lenaghan went upstairs with a flask of coffee, her tape recorder, a magazine to read, and, she also admits, a little brandy for "medicinal purposes."

She settled into the cold, uncomfortable room and accepted the fact she was not going to close the door to the room, turn out the light, or get any sleep that night. But around 2:30 in the morning, she did start to calm down a bit. Around 3 a.m., the room started to get noticeably warmer. Lenaghan said, "I thought: It's the coffee and the brandy. And then it got even warmer and I thought: No, this isn't right. And the next thing, the smell came back instantly—that same smell. And it was even stronger than before. The smell was very intense toward my head. Yes, it was a smell, but the weirdest thing of all was it was a smell that almost covered you, like a sheet—it was all-pervasive. It was almost like you could feel the smell on your clothes and in your hair and on the bed.

"I sat there for about a minute, paralyzed with fear. And I thought: Right, I'm a journalist, I've got to record a piece here—that's why I'm here. So I got my tape recorder—and apparently this was amusing when it was played back the next day, but not for me at the time. So I'm saying, 'It's 3:00 in the morning. It's gotten warmer, and the smell's just come back,' and I'm going through this and the next thing I just said, 'And I don't like it, and I'm going home!'"

Lenaghan claims she broke several Olympic sprint records that night as she darted down the very steep stone steps and back to the lobby. She said the same musty vanilla smell followed her all the way down the stairs, but stopped as soon as she crossed over to the new part of the hotel. The night manager gave Lenaghan a drink from the bar and took a very shaken BBC reporter to a room as far from the castle side of the hotel as possible, where she reluctantly spent the rest of the night.

The next morning at breakfast, the manager said the infamous door knocking went on that same evening as some of the guests in the old part of the castle complained of strange rappings. One guest even said a woman walked into her room in the middle of the night, and when the guest sat up to look closer, the woman was gone.

After breakfast, the manager told Lenaghan to go back upstairs to the Ghost Room and at least take a look at the room in daylight. Lenaghan said, "The next part may or may not have been a practical joke, and I'll never know and I don't ever want to know. After breakfast, I walked fairly gingerly up to the room, and there was no smell and it was really cold—it had been like when I first went in the night before. And we were just leaving and the manager said, 'Oh my God. Look at the mirror!' So I looked over at the mirror, and there was my name written in the dust on the mirror—'Kim.' And she said, 'I didn't do it.' I made her interrogate the staff, and they all swore that they didn't do it. I'll never know for sure, but it absolutely freaked me out."

Ballygally Castle Hotel offers a combination of old-world charm and some feisty Irish spirits. If you do happen to get a strange knock on your door in the middle of the night, do be kind to Lady Shaw—the poor girl has been through a lot.

Chapter 2:
THE RMS *QUEEN MARY*

The RMS *Queen Mary* is now permanently anchored in Long Beach, California. The ship offers overnight accommodations in its cabins and suites, dining and banquet facilities, and daily historical and ghost tours. Photo by Tony Mellard.

THE RMS *QUEEN MARY:*

Long Beach, California

Tel: 1 (562) 435-3511

Web: *www.queenmary.com*

Ghostly legends abound in ancient castles, old homes, and historic battlefields, but the supernatural is by no means only tied to land. The sea has long held stories of phantom ships with phantom sails, St. Elmo's fire, and the infamous Flying Dutchman. If we're keeping score, there is one ship that stands out above them all as having more ghosts than other ships her size had crew: The RMS *Queen Mary.*

On December 1, 1930, John Brown & Company of Clydebank, Scotland, commissioned by the Cunard Steamship Company, laid the keel of the RMS *Queen Mary.* A crew of thousands worked on the great ship's construction for just over a year. On December 11, 1931, the project was halted because of an economic depression in the United Kingdom—loans could not be secured and the funding dried up. The hull was 80 percent completed, and the ship stood nine stories high at the time. After some government backing, construction resumed on April 3, 1934. Later that same year, the Cunard Steamship Company merged with the White Star Line—the same company that owned and operated the *Titanic.* The White Star Line oversaw the completion of the new ship's construction, and on May 25, 1936, King Edward VIII, Her Majesty Queen Mary, Princess Elizabeth, the Duke and Duchess of York, the Duke and Duchess of Kent, and the Duchess of Gloucester all came to give the RMS *Queen Mary* a royal inspection.

The RMS *Queen Mary* is 1,019.5 feet long, weighs 81,237 gross tons, is 181 feet tall from its keel to the top of its smokestack, has a 160,000 horsepower engine capacity, and was built to accommodate approximately 3,000 passengers and crew comfortably. In all aspects, the *Queen Mary* is significantly bigger than the *Titanic* was, built 20 years earlier. The ship made her maiden voyage on May 27, 1936.

The *Queen Mary* was one of the last of the great transatlantic ocean liners, and her civilian service would be short-lived. In March 1940, she was painted grey and given the ominous name of the "Gray Ghost." The *Queen Mary* was pressed into service for World War II and was transporting around 15,000 troops at a time, mainly for the United States.

Psychic medium Peter James may be best known as the resident psychic on the television show *Sightings*, but he has also been investigating the history and ghosts of the *Queen Mary* since 1991. I spoke to James about the ship's ghostly history and its many fatalities. James said, "The *Queen Mary* is the most haunted place that I have ever investigated. And I've literally been around the globe with hauntings. This is number one as the most haunted place in the world. There are at least 600 active resident ghosts on the *Queen Mary*."

Why so many deaths on a luxury ocean liner? Certainly the military service has a lot to do with the fatalities. James said, "While transporting 16,000 of our troops during World War II, it was quite hot in the Indian Ocean and the *Queen Mary* was not equipped with airconditioning. Fact has it that troops were dying at a rate of one every 7 minutes for hours. That's how bad it was, because they were packed like sardines."

In addition to U.S. and allied troops, the "Gray Ghost" also picked up some German and Italian prisoners of war. James said, "The prisoners were as young as 17 years old. They were housed in the isolation ward on B deck. They chose to commit suicide rather than face the consequences of becoming prisoners of war."

In 1942, the *Queen Mary* was being escorted through hostile waters by a much smaller vessel called the *Curaçao*. The *Queen Mary* had strict orders not to stop or even slow down for any reason, as Hitler's U-boats were all around the area. The *Queen Mary* was running in a zig-zag submarine evasion pattern, and the *Curaçao* inadvertently got into the way of the great ship. The *Curaçao* was sliced in two by the

Queen Mary, and many of the more than 300 on board perished—though a few crew members were pulled from the water by other escort ships, most were lost. James said, "To this day, you can hear the collision—the residual sound effects and also the water splashing and many screams for help."

Military service doesn't account for all of the fatalities on the ship. There were medical conditions of passengers, some drownings in the pool, and even a few accidents. According to James, the ship's door number 13 features a watertight seal and can be closed, in order to section off the ship in case of a hull breach. He says at least two men throughout the ship's history were crushed to death in this doorway, and James suspects it could have been foul play.

On July 31, 1947, the *Queen Mary* returned to its peacetime mission of being a transatlantic vessel. But the days of transatlantic vessels were numbered. I spoke with Robin Wachner, the marketing communications director for the *Queen Mary*, and she shed some more light on the end of the ship's service as an ocean liner. Wachner said, "With the advent of air travel, taking the ship from Europe back to the United States was no longer really considered the way to travel. So less and less people were traveling on the *Queen Mary*, and it became more expensive to operate the ship. And she couldn't be used as a cruise ship, because she didn't have pools on the outside, as she was a transatlantic ocean liner. Everybody was taking Panamá Canal cruises, and she couldn't fit through the Panamá Canal—she's too big."

The RMS *Queen Mary* was retired from service on September 19, 1967 after completing 1,001 Atlantic crossings. The city of Long Beach, California, successfully bid to acquire the *Queen Mary* and have her permanently docked as a tourist attraction for the city of Long Beach. On December 11, 1967, she pulled in to Long Beach and has remained there ever since.

Wachner explained that, since 1967, the *Queen Mary* has operated as a hotel and has featured restaurants, catering halls, and special event tours. There are more than 365 guest rooms that are preserved exactly as they were when the ship sailed. Even some of the fixtures in the rooms are original. Today, the ship receives more than 1.4 million visitors per year.

Wachner said she's never personally experienced any ghosts onboard, but many of her colleagues have. She said, "In the marketing office, a lot of people have experienced seeing, out of the corner of their eye, a man in black. He appears almost as fast as he disappears. People have walked over to see if they can help this man, and he's just gone. We also have a lot of instances within our offices of doors just mysteriously opening and closing when there's no wind and no windows open. There have been some strange happenstances aboard the *Queen Mary* among the employees—people see disembodied heads, legs, and images, and people dressed in vintage clothing disappear into thin air."

Peter James has visited the *Queen Mary* well more than 1,000 times since 1991. His first supernatural experience onboard happened during his first tour on the ship's old "Ghosts, Myths, and Legends" tour with a friend of his. He said to his companion, "This captain just came up to me and said he was Captain Stark, and this is where they found his body. Ten seconds later, the tour guide turns around and says, 'And this is where the body of Captain Stark was found.'"

As a psychic, James certainly has an advantage in experiencing the supernatural aboard the ship, but he said there are many phenomena that have materialized for witnesses who are not psychically sensitive. He believes the first-class swimming pool is the heart of the ship, and James has encountered a significant amount of supernatural occurrences there. One such event involved the disembodied voice of a young girl named Jackie, and more than 100 witnesses experienced it at a single time. James said, "Jackie is about 4 or maybe 5 years old. After I had an interactive conversation with her, she said she would meet up with me in the other pool area. I was a bit confused, because I was only aware of one pool—the first-class swimming pool. However, in her consciousness of about 60 or more years ago, the Royal Theater used to be the second-class swimming pool, where, sadly, she drowned. Jackie speaks as clearly as we do."

Tony Mellard is a California resident who has taken Peter James's ghost tour aboard the *Queen Mary* several times. He said, "On Peter's tour, there has not been a single time I have gone and not heard voices speak, that seem to almost reverberate out of the ship itself—almost like a clanging of metal that forms itself into words. It's really bizarre. In the first-class swimming pool, I heard the infamous little "screech" that Jackie gives in response to Peter calling out to her."

On another occasion, Mellard and his wife were dining at Sir Winston's restaurant aboard the ship. Peter James explained to

Mellard and the other diners how the Sir Winston Churchill Suite was among the most haunted in the entire ship. Murmuring voices, the sound of someone clearing their throat, thumps, and bumps on the wall have all been reported emanating from the suite when it is empty. But the most prominent feature of the Churchill Suite is the smell of cigars—though smoking is not allowed anywhere on the ship. Mellard said, "Later that night, my wife and I started exploring the hallways of the ship, when we walked into the strongest smell of cigar smoke you could imagine. It just seemed to come out of nowhere, and it was literally as if someone were standing right in front of us blowing smoke right in our faces—yet we could see no visible smoke. The oddest thing about it was that the smell seemed to linger in one certain area of the middle of the hallway, and if you took one step away in any direction, it would disappear. And as soon as you stepped back, *bam*, it would overcome your sense of smell. In all our excitement, we really weren't paying attention to where we were on the ship. But in the midst of our chattering, my wife looks over to the wall, and says, 'Oh my God, look!' There was the big, golden plaque on the door—'Sir Winston Churchill Suite.' It sent chills up our spines."

On one of his tours, a woman asked Peter James if it would be okay if she brought a toy doll with a long ribbon around its neck as sort of an offering to Jackie. James said, "She put the doll on the floor, started rolling her videotape, and called out to Jackie. And then she panned her camera back, and all of a sudden on video—and I have a copy of it—the ribbon began to come undone. And it was completely pulled off the doll by Jackie."

James spoke of some common ghost sightings around the ship that many guests have reported. One encounter happened just three days prior to me speaking with him. James explained how two guests ran out of their room at 2 a.m. They claimed someone came into their rooms right through the wall of the cabin, pulled their bedding down, and turned the lights on. They fled in a panic. James claimed this was not the first time such an occurrence has taken place aboard the ship.

Through his years of psychic research on the *Queen Mary*, James has built rapport with several of the spirits onboard. One particularly tough ghost James encountered was the spirit of Sarah, whom he encounters by the swimming pool. James believes Sarah to be a middle-aged woman who drowned in the pool. He encountered this woman's spirit while trying to contact the young ghost of Jackie late one evening.

James said, "I'm saying, 'Jaaaackie...come on and talk to me, Jackie. Make your presence known.' And all of a sudden, very unexpectedly, I got slapped very hard on my right upper arm. It was summertime, so I had a short-sleeved shirt on, and it left a red mark of a hand print on my arm. This was done by Sarah. She's very aggressive, and she does not like anyone in the pool because it's her territory, so it took me a while to establish rapport with Sarah."

The *Queen Mary* is certainly a romantic and historical setting. By stepping onto her decks, visitors are transformed to another time and era where crossing the Atlantic was a very big deal that took days, not hours. History is preserved onboard the ship, as are the memories of all the action the ship has seen in both good times and bad. The energy from all that the ship has experienced reverberates through its hull and halls. With so many reported sightings by so many different people, it's possible that you, too, may experience a presence from the past onboard.

Chapter 3:
THE 1891 CASTLE INN

The 1891 Castle Inn has nine suites available for its guests. Though no formal tours are offered, you're certainly welcome to stop in and visit when you're in *N'awlins*. Photo by Andrew Craig.

THE 1891 CASTLE INN:

New Orleans, Louisiana

Tel: 1 (504) 897-0540

Web: *www.castleinnofneworleans.com*

In the Garden District of New Orleans, on a quiet side street off of St. Charles Avenue, lies the 1891 Castle Inn, a Gilded-Age mansion that seems plucked out of history. About a hundred years out of history to be exact. Walking through its halls shows visitors what the wealthy lived like in the 19th century—a time when children were seen and not heard, when your servants took care of all your needs and whims, and when you would promenade down St. Charles Avenue and only had horses, carriages, and other walkers to contend with. The mansion is so welcoming that some people who lived and worked in the house and around the property never left it...not even after they died.

Inside the 1891 Castle Inn, the 13-foot ceilings, hardwood floors, and general décor take you back to another era. The 9,500-square-foot mansion has 38 rooms (including vestibules and bathrooms), a century-old piano for guests to play, and restored furniture, but it also hosts two more relics from a bygone era—two spirits seen and experienced frequently in the house by staff members and many of the inn's guests.

The guest rooms have names like The Jazz Emporium, Napoleon, Miss Blanche's Streetcar, The Gothic Sanctuary, The Crawfish Den, and The Bordello Room. The Castle Inn's ghostly guests are encountered all over the house; however, according to co-owner Andrew Craig, the third floor seems to have the most activity.

The Castle Inn stands on land that was once a plantation in the 1800s. Before the current mansion was built, a long, wood-framed, two-story house was constructed sometime during the early to mid-1800s. The house was narrow in the front because, at the time, you were taxed on the amount of frontage facing the street. The house went back into the lot, with servants' quarters in the rear of the building. Sometime around 1891, a very prominent local man, Alva Schnitt, who was in charge of the New Orleans School District as well as a leader of a group called "The White Man's League"—a group with ideals and an agenda very similar to the Ku Klux Klan during Reconstruction times—bought the wooden house and tore it down. As a gift to his new wife, he built a three-story mansion. This community leader also died of failing health in the house.

In the 1920s, as the Great Depression was creeping into America, these New Orleans mansions were becoming too much of a financial burden for the owners. Like many others, the mansion that was to become the Castle Inn was converted to a transient rooming house. The place changed ownership several times, until the 1950s, when the Allison family took over. It would stay in the Allison family until 1998, when George Allison sold it to Andrew Craig and Karen Bacharach. The new owners renamed the mansion the 1891 Castle Inn and began extensive cosmetic work on the property.

Craig recalls the state of the mansion when they took ownership. He said, "It was disgusting. Some of the rooms he [George Allison] hadn't been into in years. Some of the rooms were lovely, some were disgusting. Fixing it up has been a labor of love."

Craig said Allison didn't mention anything about ghosts, and the new owners didn't notice any activity until they began to work on the place. Once the work began, the presence of at least two human spirits, and possibly even one ghost of a dog, became evident.

The first spirit to be seen and heard was that of a young girl who, legend has, drowned in a nearby pond that was on the plantation before the urbanization of New Orleans. Craig said, "She fell in the pond in the classic sort of petticoat, it swelled up with water, and down she went like a rock and drowned. She was wearing a pretty white dress, she was anywhere from 6 to 10 years of age, a little blond girl, and she sadly roams not just our place, but the neighborhood. Several people have told us she's looking for her mother."

The second spirit who reportedly wanders the house is that of a dashing, light-skinned black man, who was a paid servant. This gentleman was known to speak several languages, be quite fond of the ladies, and also be a bit of a drunkard. He died in his bed—he was either smoking in bed or he knocked over a heating pot and started a fire. No matter the cause, he was supposedly too drunk to escape and suffocated from the smoke. Some psychics who have visited the house believe this man haunts the inn because he feels he should be in the mansion and not the servants' quarters. One psychic woman even reported getting a ghostly kiss on the cheek from the man.

A psychic who visited the inn told Craig that there's a ghostly dog in the basement. According to Craig, "She said, 'You have a little Yorkshire Terrier ghost in your basement.' I said, 'What?!' It explains why we can hear a slight barking noise coming through the air shaft and the heating ducts in the building. We also had one of our workers claim one day that they went downstairs and heard a dog or some animal rustling around down there."

Craig told me about some of the most common occurrences in the 1891 Castle Inn. Room keys are reported missing all of the time. Craig said, "We lose more keys...we lose more stuff in this house than you'd believe!" Craig said some guests will check in, go to their rooms, and come back a few minutes later saying they don't know how, but they've already lost their room key.

Guests' wallets will end up in strange places, such as the microwave, drinking glasses will mysteriously change locations within a room when a guest goes to the bathroom, and one female guest actually had a game going with one of the ghosts. The guest told Craig that every time she put her hairbrush down on the right side of a table, as soon as she left the room and came back, it would be on the left. This went on dozens of times in only a few days.

Craig described one encounter with the ghost of the little girl that two of his guests experienced. He said, "She was seen by two women simultaneously floating in the middle of the room and trying to pull the chain on the ceiling fan. One woman turned to the other and said, 'Are you looking at what I'm looking at?' And the other woman said, 'Yes, I'm looking at the upper half of a little girl who's reaching for the chain but can't seem to quite grasp it. And the bottom half of her is cut and there's kind of misty vapors drifting down where her feet should be.' And they both watched this little girl for close to a minute floating in the middle of the room, and then she just disappeared. And they came charging downstairs saying, 'We just saw a ghost!'"

Craig himself had quite an experience with the ghost in Room 10, The Gothic Sanctuary, on the top floor. He said, "The guests tend to overpull the chain on the ceiling fan. They yank it so hard that the thing jams or the chain snaps. So I've got to change the thing. I get the ladder and I go upstairs with my little fishing tackle box, with my spare pieces and tools in it. I get on the ladder and I take the bottom part of the fan off so I can get inside the guts where the little clicker switch is, and I'm annoyed at myself because I didn't have the right part with me. Just out of habit, because we have such horrendous electric bills, I turn off the power to the light switch, and I kick my toolbox shut and lean the ladder up against the wall. The door locks itself behind you. I went downstairs, said 'hi' to the one front desk girl who is working there, went down to the basement, found the part I needed, went back upstairs no more than 7 or 8 minutes later and unlocked the door, opened it, and every single electric item that can be turned on in this three-room suite is on. The TV, the radio, the air conditioner, the two bed lamps that are independently switched, the ceiling lights, the microwave, the coffee pot, the exhaust fan, the heater, the fan in the other room, and all of the lights. So I had to go around and click them all off. I said, 'Okay, ghost. You got me on that one.'"

The ghosts at the Castle Inn are more than just pranksters. Sometimes the occurrences are a little more startling. Witnesses have reported their beds shaking, being touched by invisible hands, footprints of little invisible feet walking and jumping on the bed, and the smell of tobacco smoke.

Nicholas Franklin, the inn's former manager, told me about the only unexplained personal experience he had there: "I was staying in Room 10, and around 11:30 at night, some friends and I were watching TV, and the shower came on by itself. And not just a little bit—it was coming out full force. When we went in to check on it, the faucet was turned off. That was the only experience that I've had personally."

Franklin told me that many people do come to the Castle Inn looking for a ghostly encounter, and some get a little more than they bargained for. "I had one lady call me at 2 in the morning in tears, asking if I could come walk her out. She was staying in Room 11 [The Crawfish Den], and she said she looked over and there was a man in her bed, smoking. She was hysterically crying and said 'I don't want anything but for you to walk me out.'"

New Orleans has long been a focus of supernatural activity, and a browse through the Castle Inn's guest book proves that this bed-and-breakfast is no exception. John and Aly Brothers stayed in Room 9, Jean Lafitte's Tradewinds Hideaway, and experienced the dashing servant and little girl ghosts during their stay on July 27, 2001. An excerpt from their guest book entry reads:

The ghosts kept us up two nights in a row! The first day our TV kept coming unplugged. We'd leave and it would be unplugged when we returned. This happened a total of three times. The second night was amazing and frightening at the same time. We saw this little girl by the stairway. My wife also saw the male black ghost once or twice that night. So we finally got to sleep around 5 a.m. Oh yeah, we also heard steps running up and down our stairs—and no one else was staying on our side of the mansion that night. Around 5 a.m., the last thing we heard was a little girl giggling.

On Wednesday, September 25, 2002, Kelly Pursley of Seattle, Washington reported her experiences in Room 5, the Napoleon Room:

The hurricane was starting to move in, and we were the only ones in the house that night. Around 10:30 p.m., I heard what sounded like furniture moving. At 11:30 p.m., I heard the distinct sound of a small child's music box playing in the hall. It lasted over a minute. As soon as I laid my head down to go to sleep, I had the sensation again of a soft caress on my foot and up my leg. Sometime during the middle of the night, I woke in a daze to feel the bed moving up and down, as if someone was gently jumping on it. Quite a strange feeling! When leaving the house at 4 a.m. to catch a taxi for an early flight, my friend turned around to look up at the balcony of our room and saw a dark figure in the window watching us leave. Maybe he/she was sad to see us go?

The 1891 Castle Inn transports its visitors to another time and mindset. For the ghosts who wander its rooms and hallways, the familiarity may be why they came in the first place, but it's the energy and excitement of fresh new faces coming in and out that keeps them there. The dashing manservant, no doubt, is still looking for another lovely lady to court, while the young girl wonders if the next female guest may just be her mother.

Chapter 4:
ROSE HALL GREAT HOUSE

The Rose Hall Great House is now a museum open seven days a week from 9 a.m. to 6 p.m. The Hall can also be rented out for private functions. A gift shop and pub have been built in the former dungeon. Photo courtesy of Jamaica National Heritage Trust.

ROSE HALL GREAT HOUSE:

Montego Bay, Jamaica

Tel: 1 (876) 953-2323

Web: *www.montego-bay-jamaica.com/ajal/rosehall*

The only two times you needed to worry about Annie Palmer were when she hated you and when she loved you. Your only hope to survive her company was for her to take no notice of you at all. This was not easily accomplished if you were a slave or employee on her plantation, next to Montego Bay in Jamaica, back in the early 1800s—she felt everyone around her was at her disposal.

Better known as the White Witch of Rose Hall, Annie Palmer was as renowned for her beauty as she was for her sadistic cruelty. She tortured, mutilated, and murdered her lovers and slaves. Before she died, she vowed she would be the last mistress of Rose Hall—and its last resident. For more than 150 years, she's kept her word. Her cruel spirit still oversees the breathtaking mansion. The ghosts of those she's killed have been reported wandering the plantation and great house.

Rose Hall Plantation, built in 1770 at a cost of £30,000, was and still is a Caribbean island paradise. Annie Palmer not only enjoyed gorgeous ocean views, swaying palm trees, lush green lawns, white sand, and crystal blue ocean waters, she also lived in opulent luxury, surrounded by fine furnishings, servants, and slaves who worked the sugar cane plantation that kept her wealthy.

She was born Annie Mae Patterson to an Irish father and English mother, and the Patterson family moved to Haiti when Annie was very young. In Haiti, Annie learned voodoo from her Haitian nanny. Annie's parents mysteriously died when she was 10 years old, so she was raised by the nanny until the woman died, when Annie was 18. Annie's ambition was to gain wealth—and in the early 19th century, a woman did that by marrying rich. Annie came to Jamaica and quickly enchanted local Englishman and plantation owner, John Palmer.

The couple were married, and Annie took her position as the mistress of the plantation. She grew hungry for more wealth and excitement, and bored with her husband, she began to take an occasional lover. Being that she slept in a separate bedroom from her husband, she would demand that some of the slave men, who she fancied, come to her chamber at night. When she grew tired of her lover, or if she feared suspicions were being raised, she would either have others murder the poor slave or do it herself.

After six years of marriage, Annie knew she would inherit all of John Palmer's possessions should he pass on—and Annie was not one to wait around for nature to run its course. Annie killed John Palmer with poison, and she then closed off his bedroom and would not allow anyone to enter it again while she was alive.

The slaves had their suspicions of foul play, but they kept quiet for fear of the "White Witch," as Annie Palmer was coming to be known. Annie married and murdered two more husbands, all the while taking her slave lovers on the side, acquiring the wealth of her dead husbands, and watching slaves get flogged and beaten for her own amusement. When each husband died, she completely closed off their bedrooms; three doors were to remain closed and locked as long as Annie Palmer was the mistress of the plantation.

After the three deaths, some of the slaves started talking about the house being haunted. Doors began slamming when there was no wind to blow them shut—especially when other men came calling and fell under the enchantment of Annie.

According to Beverly Gordon, a native Jamaican and the current manager of the Rose Hall Great House, Annie Palmer not only beat the slaves in daylight but she also brought them back to the mansion for further torture. Gordon said, "Where the ladies' and gentlemen's rooms are now, that's what she used as her dungeon, and those two pits went 16 feet down. That's where she kept the slaves, if they were caught trying to run away from the property. She would get them there, throw them in the pit, and then leave them there to die without food or water, and with no medical attention whatsoever. She was gruesome, awful."

According to Gordon, the stories of the White Witch are known throughout Jamaica by many generations. She said, "Everybody knows about the Rose Hall Great House and what took place here. Children, adults, older ones, younger ones—they all know about it."

Gordon reported that Annie Palmer had so little regard for her lovers and slaves that she would send one group of slaves to go and bury the bodies of her victims and then send a second group to murder those who buried the bodies. She wanted no traces.

In December of 1831, a dashing young gentleman named Robert Rutherford from England came to Rose Hall plantation to fill the position of bookkeeper. Annie took interest in the gentleman instantly, as did her housekeeper, Millicent.

This is where the story of Rose Hall turns into a murderous soap opera that would play itself out in only a few weeks. Millicent's grandfather, Takoo, was a powerful voodoo witch and also an occasional lover of Annie Palmer. Robert Rutherford, far from the strict society of England, fancied both Millicent and his new employer, Annie Palmer. This infuriated Annie, who wanted Rutherford's attentions for herself.

The White Witch of Rose Hall cast a spell on Millicent, causing her to die within nine days. Takoo was infuriated—he stormed into the mansion and strangled Annie Palmer to death in her bed.

Annie was entombed in an above-ground, cement coffin that still sits in the east garden of the house. Some of her religious-minded former slaves tried to cast spells on her grave to keep her spirit locked up, but their magic didn't work. Annie wouldn't be stopped by death.

The house sat empty until 1905, when a family finally bought the mansion. They would not be deterred by the ghostly legends. The new owners' maid was on the balcony cleaning when she was thrown off, to her death, by an unseen force. Folklore says Annie Palmer spent a great deal of her time on the balcony, watching slaves get whipped by the overseers she commanded. Even after death, the White Witch wouldn't cease her murderous ways. The family abandoned the great mansion by Montego Bay, and it sat empty again until 1965.

In 1965, the Rose Hall Great House and all its land were purchased by U.S. entrepreneurs John and Michele Rollins. The couple spent $2.5 million restoring the house and turning it into a museum, pub, gift shop, and banquet hall. Bathrooms and a bar now stand where Annie Palmer's dungeons once loomed, but the ghost stories continue.

In 1971, a group of psychics came to Rose Hall to try and trap the spirit of Annie Palmer. Gordon said, "They tried to raise Annie, and she was giving them a hard time. She came out of the tomb, they were trying to get her back in and they could not. On her tomb, they placed three crosses on three sides. They wanted to trap her spirit back inside the tomb and they could not, so they did not put the fourth cross on. So they just left that side open."

Trapping Annie's ghost was not successful, and she still makes her presence felt in the Great House. Gordon said, "Sometimes the taps at the bar and in the kitchen start running. No one turns them on, and try as you might, you cannot get that pipe to turn off. It just comes on and goes off by itself."

Doors slam, and windows close and can't be opened no matter how hard the staff tries to push. Gordon also said that men seem to be more inclined to experience the phenomena than women. She said, "One staff member has seen a woman entering a room. He came down to ask someone who might be in there." He was startled when he was told that no one was upstairs. When he went back to look again, the woman was gone.

Gordon says some of the female staff members have caught glimpses of things, but nothing like what the male staff member experienced. Visitors have reported seeing a woman around the house, as well as the specter of a short man. Some visitors have even claimed to capture these images in their photographs.

In 2001, Jack Slater was in Jamaica for a reggae promotion he was running for his business. On the day of his trip, the weather called for rainstorms all day, which is a rarity in Jamaica. He though it was the perfect time to visit Rose Hall—not quite a dark and stormy night, but a dark and stormy day, to be certain. On his tour of the hall, Slater took several pictures—he was trying to capture a duppy (pronounced "DUH-pee," the Jamaican word for "ghost") on film. Slater said, "We got up to the room that our tour guide said was Annie Palmer's room. He said, 'This is where she did a lot of her killing.' He went through the story about how her various husbands and even some of the slaves at the plantation were killed. So as the tour went off into the next room, I said, 'Okay, this is it. This is the room which is going to have all the potential duppies in it.'"

Slater clicked some pictures of the room in general then approached a mirror on the wall opposite the bed. He said, "I looked at the mirror really carefully, because I knew if you start taking pictures of mirrors, all hell breaks loose—if you take it right in front, you get your flash right back, and it won't even come out. So my picture was taken kind of at an angle."

When Slater's picture was developed, the mirror had a foggy, ghostly scene within the frame. There is a very clear image of a woman in a white dress on the lower-left corner of the mirror and an almost jungle-like image of white, fog-like streaks. "I expected it to look kind of unusual," Slater said. "But when the film came back, there was this entire scene of stuff going on."

In a second picture he took of Annie Palmer's bed, there is a white glow on the enameled wooden bed frame, which Slater admits was his white shirt reflecting off the shiny surface. But in the picture, there is also an outline of a man's face looking down toward the bed. Could it be one of Annie Palmer's victims? Slater isn't sure he saw a ghost that day, but he does find it interesting that he set out to try and disprove that any duppies would come out on his pictures, and instead, he had not one, but two peculiar photos.

The White Witch of Rose Hall has kept her vow of being the last mistress of the plantation. Since her death, only one other family tried to live there, but they quickly fled after the death of their maid. This evil wretch of a woman who took so much pleasure in watching others suffer is now stuck wandering the hallways and walkways of the mansion that she once ruled over with a wicked hand. Annie Palmer is the stuff of nightmares to the children of Jamaica, and according to many witnesses, the nightmare of the White Witch is not over.

Chapter 5:
HIBBING HIGH SCHOOL

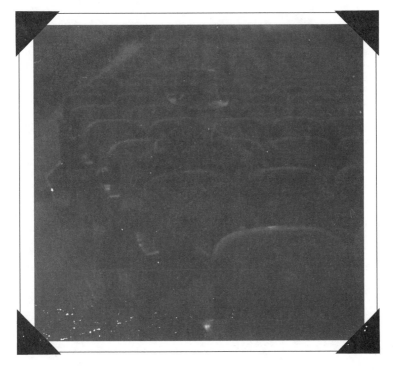

Is this the stage manager from the high school's early days? Hibbing High School houses grades 7 through 12 and serves the greater Hibbing area. Though no formal tours are offered, there are many school and community productions that offer access to its impressive and haunted auditorium. Photo by Chuck Perry.

HIBBING HIGH SCHOOL:

Hibbing, Minnesota

Tel: 1 (218) 263-3675

Web: *www.hibbing.k12.mn.us/2hhs/hhs_welcome.htm*

TOP SECRET

In northern Minnesota, about 80 miles northwest of Duluth and located on the iron range, an almost medieval-looking castle rises against the skyline. At first glance, you wouldn't know the spires and elaborate protrusions of the façade actually enclose a high school—the most opulent high school that steel money could buy in 1920. The extravagance doesn't end on the outside by any means. From marble staircases and brass railings to art deco walls, this place is like no high school I've ever seen. But if this educational kingdom has a crowning jewel, it's the auditorium. Modeled after New York City's Capitol Theater, many details of this great room, such as its woodwork, engravings, artwork, and crystal chandeliers, make this a place that will take your breath away. The auditorium is also the home of legends—both the musical kind as well as the ghost of seat J47, who has been known to make an occasional appearance for the camera.

Hibbing, Minnesota, is a blue-collar town. Generations have toiled pulling iron ore from the ground in the area's steel mines ever since mining explorer Frank Hibbing set foot on the land in 1892. Within a year of its discovery, people were moving to town in droves for the job opportunities of working in the mines. By July of 1893, a 2-square-mile town site had been laid out and was given the name of Superior. The little town was on a fast-track to growth. The name Superior was changed to Hibbing in honor of its founder less than 15 years after its incorporation. Town residents were grateful to Mr. Hibbing for his discovery that led to steady work for so many.

By 1914, Hibbing's economy was booming—it had been called the "richest village in the world." The assessed valuation of this village was more than $84 million. This steel town was getting a lot of luxuries from the profits of Oliver Mining Company, a subsidiary of U.S. Steel Corporation.

Hibbing is also known as the town that moved. As 1920 arrived, large deposits of iron ore were being discovered in the midst of residential neighborhoods. The mining company was buying all of the property it could, but eventually whole neighborhoods were going to have to be moved. In exchange for the major inconvenience of relocating houses (at the company's expense), Oliver Mining Company proposed the building of a grand high school.

Initial construction on Hibbing High School began on April 28, 1920, when a building contract was awarded to Jacobson Brothers Construction. The initial cost was $3,927,325. In 1922, a stage manager named Bill was brought in from New York to run the impressive auditorium (I'm withholding Bill's last name, as he still has family who work at the school). Bill loved the theatre and loved overseeing the performances in this impressive piece of New York, cloned and placed in northern Minnesota.

The Hibbing auditorium held vaudeville performances, symphony orchestras, and school plays. The school was initially built in the shape of a capital "E" and would house grades ranging from kindergarten through a two-year junior college. It also housed several spirits who still haunt the building but seem to focus most of their attention on the auditorium.

Ghost stories are not the only legends that come from the Hibbing High School auditorium. Folk rock singer Robert Zimmerman (better known as Bob Dylan) made one of his first public performances on the auditorium stage during a talent show when he was a student there. Zimmerman was a graduate of the Hibbing High School class of 1959.

Today, Hibbing is a town of 17,000 people. The heyday of the iron mines has past, though a few are still open and employ some of the locals.

Chuck Perry has been the Stage Manager at Hibbing High School since 1979. I spoke with him about the ghost stories he's heard in the school, and about the remarkable photos he's taken of the ghost in seat J47. Perry has been living in Hibbing most of his 49 years and said he heard about the ghosts even before he started working at the high school. He's well-known in the community and was a bit hesitant at first to talk about the ghosts.

Some of the rumors behind the ghost stories that have gone around the high school include someone falling off the balcony and dying, one of the chandeliers falling on a person in the seats below, a physically disabled student with health problems expiring in the auditorium, and the death of the auditorium's first stage manager, Bill. Chuck Perry was able to verify the story of the disabled girl dying in the auditorium to be true, and Bill did pass away in the 1940s. The others, he was not able to verify.

Photo by Chuck Perry.

Perry explained how Hibbing High School is a mecca for Bob Dylan fans, and during the summers, the town has a Dylan festival. Perry recalled one incident in the early 1990s when a devoted Dylan fan and apparent New-Ager walked into the auditorium. Perry said, "She walks around the rows of seats, and she mentions something about a chill. And I said, 'Yeah, okay, sure.' Pretty soon she starts talking about this seat J47 specifically. She says she can feel something there."

Perry dismissed the event until shortly after he saw a special on an educational cable channel about people who go into graveyards trying to photograph ghosts. Perry thought he'd try his hand at spirit photography and use seat J47 as his test. Perry said, "I took an old Polaroid [camera] that I had backstage—basically it was a prop. I went and bought some film for it, and I set it up on a tripod right at seat J47. I took a few pictures, and basically nothing happened. I tried it a few more times and took about 50 pictures total. Six of them came out with something in them."

As others around the state have heard about the ghost of seat J47, they too have brought their cameras to try and capture something. Perry told me about a woman from the Minnesota Special Education Department who took a few pictures of the seat while Perry looked on. Perry said, "She used a digital camera and she took a picture of the seat. She didn't get an image in the seat, but she got a flare, like a light flare. So she took two pictures. I thought the first one was just a fluke, and when the second one came out the same way, well, she was just petrified."

The most profound of the six pictures Perry took can be seen at the beginning of this chapter. You can see a semi-translucent man wearing a hat and sitting in seat J47, which is located in the center section of seats, on the right side of that section if you're facing the stage. The seat has some people spooked. Perry said, "There's kids that come here that won't sit there. They don't even want to walk by it."

Perry has also had a few unexplained experiences within the auditorium. He told me about one incident that took place in 1999. He said, "I'm on stage, and I'm cutting some plywood for a set we're building. I've got a power saw out there, and I've got music playing. I finished the piece I was working on, and I walked back into the stage office to get a cup of coffee. I dust the sawdust off me and sit down for a minute. Literally, a minute or two. I walked back on the stage, and my saw was on the other side of the stage. I was working stage left and I came back out, and my wood and everything was on stage left, but my power saw was stage right, plugged into the other outlet on the other side. I'm thinking somebody is messing with me. I unplug it, bring it back, plug it in, start up the saw, and all of a sudden it shuts off. There was a short in the actual cord on the saw itself. So I thought maybe somebody's trying to tell me something here—I don't know."

On November 26, 1996, Hibbing High School fell victim to a significant amount of smoke damage due to a fire that broke out when some remodeling work was being done on the west wing of the building. The school would remain closed for more than a month for repairs. Perhaps the spirit in the auditorium was watching out that there wasn't another fire?

The first story Perry ever heard about ghosts in the auditorium involved the backstage area. Perry said the encounter took place in the mid-1970s, before he started working at the high school. He said, "We have 10 dressing rooms, and one of them is really large. Supposedly this gal was back there getting her makeup on before the show. Somebody walked in the dressing room she assumed was in costume, she looked up, and they just kind of were gone. And that happen two or three times in that room."

A janitor at the school, who wished to remain nameless, claims to have heard someone enter a classroom behind him when he was cleaning the room one night. Every time he turned around to look, he heard footsteps move back into the hall. When he turned back to his work, the steps returned. He never saw anything, but he certainly heard the footsteps.

People from all over Minnesota have heard about the ghosts in Hibbing High School. One Hibbing resident who has actually investigated the hauntings is Hibbing resident Brian Leffler. Leffler is the founder of the Northern Minnesota Paranormal Investigators (NMPI), and his group explored the auditorium in January of 2004.

Leffler explained a specific sense he gets when he's in the presence of a ghost. He said, "I'm not really psychically sensitive per se, but what I get is what feels like a chill. It's almost like a small electrical charge. Like when you were a kid, did you ever put your tongue on a 9-volt battery? It feels like that, but it starts in my neck and runs all the way down my spine to my butt. I get that chill when I'm in the presence of a spirit. When that chill meter goes off, something's going on, and they're around me."

Leffler got that chill when he walked into the main dressing rooms backstage in the auditorium. He said, "I walked in there, and my chill shot up into my jaw and my neck. That means pretty much that I'm being touched by one [a spirit] at that point. What I could see almost looked like a red, hazy outline of an upper body right in front of me. It was weird; it was only there for a second. It was almost like a fog. It was at that very instant when I got my chill."

Leffler had his 35mm camera with him, ready to try and capture the ghost on film. He saw that the bright-green "flash-ready" light was on, so he lifted up his camera and tried to take a picture of the red mist in front of him. He said, "I snapped a picture, and the flash did not go off. The camera advanced, but the flash didn't go off. When I got the picture back, the picture has the date on it, but it's full of lines. It's not black, it's full of lines like interference on your TV. Normally in a dark room without a flash, it would just be black."

In addition to taking pictures and videotaping the investigation, NMPI also set up audio recording devices to try to record Electronic Voice Phenomena (EVP)—audio captured via a process where paranormal researchers allow a tape recorder to record a quiet room. Sometimes, when the tape is played back later, voices that were not audible to the human witness will be heard on the tape. Leffler said, "In the first minute of taping, we have at least half a dozen distinct voices that aren't us. One of them says, 'We're waiting for Frank.' It's just amazing. The place is haunted by quite a few spirits."

Hibbing High School is an impressive piece of architecture. Money wasn't the only thing that built the institution—it was the workers who painstakingly sculpted every corner and the teachers who made education their life's wcrk. School spirit isn't just about the crowd cheering for their football team; sometimes it's about the very people who studied and worked there, just because they loved the place. If I were attending a production in Hibbing High School's grand auditorium, I would avoid seat J47 out of respect, but I would very much like the seat right next it. Maybe I would catch a glimpse or a few words from a real school spirit.

Chapter 6:
THE DEANE HOUSE

The Deane House Restaurant is open Monday through Friday, 11 a.m. to 3 p.m., and Saturday and Sunday, 10 a.m. to 3 p.m. Additionally, the building is available for private functions, "murder mystery" dinners, and is also used by some programs offered by the Fort Calgary Preservation Society. Photo courtesy of Fort Calgary.

THE DEANE HOUSE:

Calgary, Alberta

Fort Calgary

Tel: 1 (403) 269-7747

Web: *www.fortcalgary.com/deane.htm*

The Deane House is a house that got around—literally. The entire building would be moved twice and gather some gruesome history along its short but colorful journeys. Murders, suicides, and even a few natural deaths would lead to a slew of future ghost activities for this early cornerstone of Calgary.

The city of Calgary in Alberta can trace its start to a small outpost called Fort Calgary that was established in 1875 in response to the lawless whiskey traders in the region. At the junction of the Bow and Elbow rivers, Fort Calgary was the base of the North West Mounted Police. A few years later, the railway reached the fort and a town was born. As the region grew in population, the fort grew with it. In 1906, a stately manor was constructed in the fort for Superintendent Captain Richard Deane. Deane felt the quarters used by the previous superintendent weren't good enough for his wife, Martha. At a cost of $6,200 to build, Deane would say that his new home was "Certainly the best house in Mounted Police occupancy at that date."

Martha Deane never got to see the new home. She died of illness in the town of Lethbridge in southern Alberta. By 1914, the fort closed, the land was sold to the Grand Trunk Pacific Railway, and Captain Deane retired to his native England. Grand Trunk tore down all of the Fort Calgary buildings with the exception of the Deane House, which was spared to become the station agent's quarters. Later that same year, the Deane House made its first move from its original location, at the corner of what is now 9th Avenue and 6th Street Southeast, to the southeast corner of the property.

In 1929, the house was sold to local entrepreneur C.L. Jacques, who would move it again—this time boats and giant flotation devices were used to move the structure across the Elbow River to its opposite bank. The feat was so remarkable that it made a 1930 issue of *Popular Mechanics* magazine. Many speculated that Jacques would have saved money had he simply built a new home on the other side of Elbow River.

After the second relocation of the Deane House, it became a boarding house and entered the darkest chapter of its existence.

Bob Pearson is the Interpretation Coordinator for Fort Calgary and has worked at the fort since 2000. Pearson is a Calgary native who has heard about the ghosts of the Deane House since he was a child. "Folks in Calgary may not know anything else about the Deane House, and they may not know anything else about Fort Calgary, but they do know that the Deane House is haunted," Pearson said. The ghost stories are so well-known that Pearson has had to incorporate them into the educational programs he runs for area school children. The staff at Fort Calgary has learned through experience that, if the ghosts are not talked about, the children will inundate the guides with questions about the supernatural residents anyway.

I spoke to Pearson about some of the history and ghosts of the house. During the period when the building was a boarding house, the Deane House had a seedy reputation. Pearson said, "During the Second World War, it was off-limits to military personnel. To let you know what kind of a house it was, people boarded there for maybe an hour at a time." There were murders, suicides, and at times, it was reported to be a house of ill repute.

In 1933, a 14-year-old boy and his father were tenants in the Deane House. The boy was epileptic and was scorned by other children for his occasional seizures. The dismayed boy committed suicide in the attic of the house. Ten years later, in 1943, the building changed ownership from C.L. Jacques to Alex Brotherton, who continued operating the home as a boarding house and often sat in the parlor and whiled away the time, smoking his pipe.

A murder/suicide took place in the Deane House, in 1952, when a husband stabbed his wife to death and then took his own life, as their two children watched in horror. Brotherton's daughter, Alfena Cunningham, who lived with Brotherton, died in the house of natural causes in 1965. Three years later, Brotherton passed on, also of natural causes.

Deaths in the Deane House occurred from 1933 and ended in 1968 with the death of Alex Brotherton. There are other unconfirmed reports of murder at the Deane House, including one man who was allegedly shot on the front porch and another killed inside the house. After Brotherton's death, the house fell into disrepair until the city stepped in.

In 1973, the city of Calgary bought the Deane House as a restoration project for their upcoming centennial celebration in 1975. In 1975, the newly restored building would be an artist's studio and then a teahouse until the early 1980s, when it was transformed into a preserved historic site and restaurant. It was in the 1960s and 70s that the haunted reputation began to grow.

According to Barbara Smith's book, *Ghost Stories of Alberta* (Hounslow Press, 1993), an exorcism was performed in the early 1990s at the Deane House. However, by the many accounts reported since, we must assume the exorcism didn't work.

In the late 1990s, local television station CFCN hired a psychic to come check out the building. In the segment, the psychic claimed there were two spirits definitely living in the house—one on the front porch and the other one in the parlor. The psychic also believed the house was built on native Indian burial ground.

The spirit of a native man has been reported at least twice inside the house. Pearson said, "One time, someone was here for murder mystery dinner and she went down in the basement. She came back up and said there was an old native guy with braids who told her that she shouldn't be here and that the site was sacred."

According to Pearson, the parlor has a noticeably higher frequency of supernatural phenomena. Today, the parlor is the bar section of the restaurant, and even when the bar is empty, staff and patrons occasionally smell pipe smoke, though no one is seen smoking. And there are accounts of witnesses who have seen the ghost of Mr. Brotherton sitting with his pipe.

People also report hearing things in the parlor. Pearson said, "There was an old telephone that wasn't connected to anything. Not only is it not connected, I've discovered there's nothing inside it—it doesn't have any inner workings. Some people reported that they could hear the phone ring. They go in and try to answer it, and of course there is no one there."

The attic of the Deane House is an additional hot spot for ghost activity. Pearson explained that there are two cupboards in the attic space on the Fort Calgary side of the house. He said, "The one on the right-hand side we use for school programming—costumes, props, and things like that. And in the cupboard on the other side, there is a stain on the left-hand side of the cupboard's floor, which some people say looks like blood. My cousin, who is a doctor, says it doesn't look like blood. It's very hard to take off—they've tried to scrub it off, but it doesn't really come off. I don't know what it is. It's reported to be a bloodstain, and some people say the stain gets larger and smaller at different times."

Corinne Schneidmiller has been working as the Banquet Supervisor for the Deane House and for Fort Calgary since 2002. Schneidmiller learned about the ghosts her first day on the job, when her boss brought her around for a tour and told her some of the legends. Schneidmiller has heard footsteps upstairs, when she knows no one is on the second floor, and has also smelled the pipe smoke. She believes some subtle yet unexplained event occurs almost every day, but she had an encounter in the summer of 2003 in the basement of the Deane House that she will never forget.

Schneidmiller said, "I went downstairs to put some stuff away in our cooler, and just out of the corner of my eye, I saw something. There were three rows of stacked chairs, and I looked over and saw a very distinct outline of a native gentleman standing in the middle row of chairs. I could see chairs in front of him and chairs behind him, and he was standing in the chairs. I couldn't really see him from the knee down. He was wearing a long-sleeved shirt with a collar and a vest over top, and he had a long braid. He was looking up and out the window, so I saw his left profile. And then he turned and looked right at me and I ran upstairs."

On another occasion, Schneidmiller was in the Deane House with two of the cooks, who were busy in the kitchen. One of her servers had run over to Fort Calgary to get some ice, because the ice machine was broken in the restaurant, when she heard something upstairs. She said, "I heard our piano playing upstairs. It's actually an antique, and no one is supposed to play it. And I'm thinking there shouldn't really be anybody here. It was beautiful music being played from that piano. I'm a piano player myself, and I thought it's going to be really mean to go tell them to stop. So I go upstairs to tell whoever it is that's playing the piano not to, because it's an antique. And as I'm walking up the stairs, I got to about the second step from the top and they stopped playing. I heard the piano bench being pushed back under, and then I heard footsteps walking away from the piano. As I walked to the entrance of the room where the piano was, I heard the footsteps as they walked right past me. And I kind of felt a little bit of a whoosh of air. Like someone walking briskly beside you. But I never saw anything. They obviously heard me coming up the stairs and decided they were done playing."

Staff members have been experiencing strange sightings and events in the restaurant for many years. Bob Pearson remembered one experience a former manager of the restaurant relayed. He said, "The former manager, Robert, was sitting there one night and thinking about going home and then figured, 'No, I'll stay and do the books,' when he claimed that his backpack had sort of levitated off of a shelf and come down at his feet. He said when that happened, he decided then that he would go home."

Another staff member who worked in the building, when it was a teahouse in the late 1970s, claimed to have seen a man in a black cloak, who was very solid, walk down the stairs, but the man seemed to vanish below the knees. The dark gentleman walked down the stairs, past the shocked waiter, and out the front door and disappeared.

Considering all of the macabre and ghostly history of the Deane House, would it bother you to work in such a place? Schneidmiller said, "Not so much, unless I'm alone. As soon as I know I'm alone, my hair stands on end. When I'm the last to leave, I'll lock up—that just involves walking to the front door, locking it, and turning out the lights as I go back to the back door. From the front door to the back door is maybe 20 feet, and I run, because I've seen and heard quite a few things—and though it doesn't scare me as much as it used to, I don't think I'll ever get used to it."

Chapter 7:
IMPERIAL CASINO HOTEL

The Imperial Casino Hotel features lodging, dining, and gambling. Though no formal ghost tours are offered, many of the staff have had a run-in with George, the hotel's only permanent resident. Photo by Paula Duwe.

IMPERIAL CASINO HOTEL:

Cripple Creek, Colorado

Tel: 1 (719) 689-7777

Web: *www.imperialcasinohotel.com*

George Long never heard his daughter coming when she followed him to the top of the Imperial Hotel's basement stairs carrying an iron skillet. History is unclear whether the blow from the frying pan or the subsequent fall down the rickety stairs did him in, but the end result was indisputable: George Long was dead—though definitely not forgotten. George would never allow that.

In October of 1890, a man named Bob Womack made a discovery that turned a small gulch in Colorado, whose residents consisted mostly of cattle, into a city of more than 25,000 people in the span of only a few years. Cripple Creek is a town born from the gold rush. And when talking about gold, it didn't get any richer than Cripple Creek— more than $600 million in this precious metal was discovered in the area—making it the biggest find on the planet. Hotels, theaters, and saloons sprouted up to give the miners a place to spend their gold. The lifestyles of the workers and cowboys were usually more than the law could handle. Homicides, mining accidents, and lynchings were a part of early Cripple Creek's daily life.

Maybe it was the thin air? The town sits at 9,494 feet above sea level. To give you an idea of the altitude, planes that fly above 10,000 feet are required by the Federal Aviation Administration (FAA) to use supplemental oxygen. Maybe the atmosphere conspired with the minds and spirits of town residents to fuel tempers and spawn hallucinations. Maybe it was something more.

The Imperial Hotel was built in 1896, during the reconstruction of Cripple Creek, after two fires had completely leveled the town, doing over $2 million in damage, killing six people, and leaving more than 5,000 homeless. Originally named The Collins Hotel (Mrs. E.F. Collins, Proprietor), the establishment changed hands several times in its first decade of operation. The building became known as the New Collins Hotel around the turn of the century, then the Imperial Hotel between 1905 and 1910. It was during this time period that an Englishman named George Long took ownership.

Long was born to English aristocrats, though according to some sources, his deafness made him an embarrassment to the family, so they shipped him off to America. Another source says George married his first cousin—an act that further shunned him from his family.

Under George Long's ownership, the Imperial flourished. George and his wife had two children; a daughter was the first born, followed several years later by their son. The family lived in an apartment located off the main lobby of the Imperial, which today is the Red Rooster Bar.

As Cripple Creek grew up and the rich veins of gold drastically slowed in their production, the first boom period for the area ended. But the Long family pressed on with their hotel, hoping better times were ahead.

As George Long's daughter got older, it became more apparent that she had a mental disability. Arguments would ensue when the girl went into fits, and the remedy was usually locking her in the apartment so she didn't disturb other guests. But one argument, in the late 1930s, threw Long's daughter over the edge. She followed George to the rickety, steep pine steps leading to the basement coal bin and killed her father. She was institutionalized for her crime.

In 1946, Wayne and Dorothy Mackin bought the Imperial Hotel from George Long's widow. I spoke to Stephen Mackin, who was born in Cripple Creek in 1947 and spent the first seven years of his life living in the same apartment George Long and his family lived in. During the time the Mackin family owned the Imperial, they worked to bring theater back to Cripple Creek, both for the cultural aspect as well as for a business draw for their hotel. By 1953, the Mackins were producing turn-of-the-century melodramas on Imperial's stage. Cripple Creek's second boom was beginning; the tourists were coming.

Stephen Mackin definitely believes the spirit of George was present where he lived and worked. He said, "The things that we did see from George were all friendly things. There was nothing that was spooky or evil or anything like that." Over the years, George became the classic ghostly scapegoat. When little things went wrong like doors slamming, drawers getting stuck, or stereos going on the fritz, whether supernatural or not, they were blamed on George. But there were those who did see and experience George at the Imperial Hotel.

Mackin was able to shed further light on the life of George Long. Stephen described a man who was a painter of landscapes and settings from his native England and from around Cripple Creek (Mackin himself owns more than 20 original George Long paintings). Long was an architect, as well, but also a bit of a lush, who was known for liking his Scotch whiskey a bit too much—and he had a temper to match his habit.

Author, astrologer, and psychic Linda Goodman lived a block away from the Imperial Hotel and was friends with Stephen Mackin. Mackin claimed Goodman often came to the Imperial and psychically communicated with George.

"I'm sure that George is still there somehow," Mackin said. "Nobody in my immediate family ever saw him, but I had a director for my theater that saw him, I had a couple of actors that saw him, I had a couple of people who worked in the kitchen who also saw him."

Mackin described one of the more profound George sightings, one that took place in the early 1980s. He said, "I had a guy named Pat Sawyer who was an actor with us and he saw George as sure as the dickens in the theater one afternoon. When he went down there to open up the bar, George was standing behind the bar. I asked what he looked like and he gave me a description. The description matched a lot of what we had heard George looked like." It was that of a well-dressed man with a mostly bald head except for a ring of monk-like hair circling the base.

The Mackins never promoted their ghost because of their concern of who the legends would draw in to the building. Stephen reported seeing people sitting in the middle of the third floor hallway holding a séance with a Ouija board. "It just attracted kind of strange folks," Mackin said.

In 1992, gambling came to Cripple Creek. Hotels could become casinos and the Mackin family sold the Imperial. The new owners got to work renovating to fit the new casino and restaurant. "I think during the time they did major reconstruction on the building that may have upset him [George]," Mackin said.

Since the renovation, the Imperial Casino and Hotel has been restored to its Victorian splendor, complete with hand-painted wall-paper from France, antique furnishings, and priceless crystal chandeliers. The hotel setting offers a stark contrast to its noisy and bright casino.

Supernatural phenomena picked up in the 1990s. Richard L. Duwe was an employee of the casino from 1994 to 1997. He worked various jobs at the casino including porter, security guard, and slot machine technician. Duwe's first job was working as a porter on the graveyard shift. The casinos in Cripple Creek close at 2 a.m., so all is quiet for six hours until they are allowed to open again. Duwe was told of a peculiar encounter involving a slot machine. He said, "According to what a security guard was telling me, the motor kicked off in the hopper and it proceeded to dump every coin out into the bowl. This was about 4:00 in the morning. And it's physically impossible for that to happen."

Duwe explained how modern computerized slot machines have multiple fail-safes to ensure that if the machine does malfunction, first an electric lock kicks in to hold the coins inside, plus a mechanical lock for back-up. Yet the security camera in the casino showed a vacant machine just empty several hundred dollars worth of coins. When the Colorado gaming commission examined the machine they were not able to find anything wrong with it. Perhaps George wasn't happy about a casino in his beloved hotel?

Duwe personally experienced another slot machine mishap after the place had closed for the evening. In the silent casino he and several others heard the familiar *ding* of a slot machine accepting a coin for play. Duwe got on the radio to notify security that possibly a customer had managed to stay inside after closing and was using a machine. After searching the hundreds of machines in the casino they couldn't find the phantom customer, nor a machine with its "coin accepted" light illuminated.

On another occasion, Duwe was working overnight security in a room called "Hard Count." This was the room that contained the machines that rolled loose coins from the slot machines. It's a noisey room with a lot of whirring machines and tinkling coins. This room is separated from the rest of the hotel by two sets of doors and a small hallway for security reasons. Duwe was in the room when he heard a knock on the door. The knock turned into the sounds of slams, as if someone was kicking the door. He ran out to investigate but found the area empty. The only (living) people it could have been was the cleaning crew, but after a quick call on his radio, Duwe learned the entire cleaning crew was in their break room eating lunch, and they had all been there for at least 15 minutes. When he returned to the Hard Count room, he yelled "Knock it off, George!" A trick he and others have learned that will stop George's antics—at least for a little while.

"I think everybody that worked there—at least on the night shift—has at least one George story to tell," Duwe said.

Rick Wood runs Cripple Creek Ghost Walk Tours, and he told me about some of George's prankster habits within the Imperial Hotel. "He still wanders the halls," Wood said. "There's a few rooms—I think 39 and 42 are reasonably active. He [George] opens and closes doors and leaves, the water on in the sinks. One of his fun tricks is to pull the drawer out of the dresser and leave it there. And when you go to turn the water off, you run into the drawer."

Cripple Creek is a hot spot for supernatural activity. Many of the buildings in town have a ghostly legend attached to them. The more people I spoke with, the more I heard of other haunted buildings. I asked Duwe why the town was so haunted. He said, "In my opinion, the whole town is inherently evil. The Ute Indians that were native to that area considered that particular area sort of off-limits. They felt that evil spirits hung out there." Duwe admits when he visits Cripple Creek today, he doesn't particularly like to be there—especially after dark.

George Long belonged at the Imperial Hotel. His family shunned him back in England, but in his hotel he was king of his castle. He was free to paint and to run his business—his way. It's not much of a surprise that George still wants to supervise the goings on at the Imperial.

Chapter 8:
THE CATACOMBS MUSEUM

The Catacomb Museum is open daily except for Mondays and bank holidays. Call for hours of operation. Tours are self-guided, though museum staff is available to answer questions. Photo by Jeff Belanger.

THE CATACOMBS MUSEUM:

Paris, France

Tel: 33 (0) 1-43-22-47-63

Web: *www.paris.org/Musees/Catacombes/info.html*

TOP SECRET

"Avez-vous vu un fantôme?" I asked the man at the ticket counter in my best French if he has seen a ghost. "Je ne sais pas," was his reply. The man smiled and shrugged his shoulders. When in Paris, France, you have your choice of world-class museums. The Louvre is an obvious choice, Musee d'Orsay is another well-known place, but there is one Paris museum that's as haunted as it is macabre. You won't find it on the Champs-Elysees; in fact, you won't find it above ground at all. To get to the Catacombs, you'll be traveling more than 20 meters below the city streets in the Montparnasse section of Paris.

There are human bones stacked in the tunnels under the city—a lot of them. But I wasn't prepared for just how many there would be. I was ready to hear more accounts of the moving shadows and ghostly voices that have been reported throughout the centuries in those bowels of Paris, but I wasn't ready for how the experience would make me feel.

The Catacombs of Paris are a network of tunnels and caves that run for more than 300 kilometers under the city. To build a city, you need materials. The Romans were the first to quarry the limestone in the area in 60 B.C.E.; however, those quarries were the open-air kind— the Romans just dug out the rock that was exposed. As the city grew and covered the landscape, tunneling would be required to get more building materials. In 1180 C.E., Philippe-Auguste became King. He was a major proponent of tunneling to quarry in order to build ramparts to protect the city, and it was under his rule that this tunnel network was truly born.

The quarries grew in size and complexity and produced building materials for centuries to come. Quarrying continued with reckless abandon until problems began to arise. In the 18th century, the city of Paris (and the weight of its buildings) continued to grow as the ground became more hollow underneath. Some buildings began to collapse and fall into the earth that was opening up below them. On April 4, 1777, the *Inspection Générale des Carrières* was formed to manage, fill in, or close sections of the tunnels deemed dangerous.

It was during the 18th century that a second problem arose for Parisians: The graveyards were getting full—very full. The *Cimetière des Innocents* (Cemetery of the Innocent) alone held more than 30 generations of human remains.

Taara, as she is known in the Paris underground, is the author of a French Website on the Catacombs, *www.chez.com/taara/*. She explained to me, "Families used to pay the parish priest to bury their dead in here [the cemetery near the church]. The priest didn't want to refuse money, so after a while, of course, there's no more [room]. So many priests decided to build a sort of house for dead people, which is called a 'charnier' [mass grave]. The dead accumulated there."

As the emerging city enclosed around the cemeteries, there was no place to go but up. Near the end of the life of the Cemetery of the Innocent, as well as several other cemeteries, the ground swelled more than 10 feet above the road. The smell was tormenting those who lived in close proximity to the graveyard. Some of the cemetery walls actually broke open, spilling rotting bodies onto the streets and into the cellars of some adjacent buildings. Soon after, disease took hold of those living in the vicinity, and people began dying from the pestilence spread by the corpses. The decision was made to start emptying the cemetery and to place the bones into the network of tunnels under the city. In 1785, when the bones were moved to the underground network en masse, the quarries became the Catacombs.

Disturbing the dead is a bit of a universal taboo. It's understood across many cultures that one should leave the dead alone, and many go through great care to perform rituals and ceremonies to see off their departed loved ones to the afterlife. However, the living will usually take precedence over the bodies of their kin who have passed on.

Located off the Denfert-Rochereau Metro stop, the Catacomb Museum exists to oversee the tunnels and bones, to teach the history of why the bones are there, and to provide the only means to visit the mortal remains of more than 1,000 years of Parisians. For €5 (euros), visitors can descend into the Catacombs.

A spiral cement staircase leads visitors down 130 steps, to 20 meters below the surface. At the bottom of the stairs, there are two rooms full of photographs of ancient graffiti from within the Catacombs as well as some of the below-ground structures. After passing through the two small rooms, you'll enter the actual Catacombs. The ceiling of the tunnel is as low as 6 feet and as high as about 12 feet on average, though some sections have an almost cathedral-looking structure high above your head. The lighting is very low, but your eyes adjust.

The limestone walls are tan in color and cool to the touch. The fine gravel under your feet crunches with each step, and the only other sound is an occasional drip-drip from somewhere in the tunnels. Parts of the ceiling collect water in an upside-down puddle, and when the water gets too heavy, it drips on an unsuspecting passerby or to the ground.

Along the walls there are dated carvings and graffiti spray-painted in French. The tunnel makes 90-degree right and left turns, and in this part of the Catacombs, the environment feels like a tunnel in the rock—nothing more. You may begin to wonder if you're in the right place at all. After a few more long tunnels, rights, and lefts, visitors will approach some painted pillars surrounding a narrow doorway. The sign on top reads: "Arrete! C'est ici L'Empire de la Mort"—"Stop! Here is the Empire of the Dead." Due to the difference in darkness between the two rooms, you can't see what is in the tunnel beyond until you walk through. It's a good idea to pause here for a moment before passing into the Ossuary of Denfert-Rochereaux, what lies on the other side is overwhelming.

In a passage no more than 6 to 8 feet in width are stacks of human bones and skulls. At the doorway they are stacked about four feet high. The skulls greet those who enter with empty but powerful stares. All around you there is nothing but the ornate patterns of bones and skulls as far down the tunnel as light will allow you to see. Within the entire Catacombs, there are more than 6 million bodies stored—only bones now. Though some bones can be found in the Catacombs in other parts of Paris, most of the bones are housed in the 1.7-kilometer stretch that the Catacomb Museum manages.

In different sections, the skulls form patterns within the stacks of arm and leg bones. There are skull crosses, hearts, arcs, and other groupings. The stacking of bones is intricate, symmetrical, and very macabre. Try to imagine how the people who had to stack these bones must have felt. Dumping millions of human remains down a 20-meter hole is not very respectful of the dead. Perhaps the meticulous care in the arrangement of the remains was the workers' way of trying to give some dignity and beauty to the deceased.

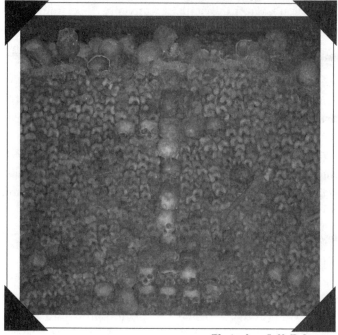

Photo by Jeff Belanger.

All along the 1.7 kilometers of tunnels, there are off-shoots that are barred so visitors can't get lost—1.7 kilometers is only a tiny fraction of the overall network. Taara said, "In the nonofficial Catacombs, the bones are not placed as you've seen them. They are not well-ordered. They are just accumulated in a little gallery. So you have to crawl on them. It's a very strange sensation, but after a while, it's not really different than crawling on rocks." Taara has been a "cataphile" for 17 years. In her younger days, she went into the tunnels several times a week. Now with her job and family, she still gets down below once a month.

In different lengths of tunnel, there are signs marking which cemetery the particular bones came from, along with the date they were placed. The process started in 1785, and the oldest year marked in the museum is 1859. Though the movement of bones to the Catacombs wasn't a nonstop process, for at least seven decades bones were being transferred below ground.

Photo by Jeff Belanger.

Taara explained, "You can find bones in a very small part of the Catacombs. The most interesting thing is that those quarries are the witness of a great part of history. For example, you can still see traces of the Revolution or other important periods like the Second World War. You can see many places that are fabulously architected, the sort of architecture you can't find now. So it's really a very lovely place, and we are proud to know those places because most Parisian people do not know there's another Paris under Paris."

"It's a little overwhelming with all of the bones," said Julie Hardman of Tempe, Arizona. I spoke with Hardman after she visited the museum with her daughter, Megan.

A security guard who asked not to be identified told me, "Some people go down and they are very afraid after seeing the bones. Some say they hear things. Voices."

The lights are very dim in the tunnels, and as your body blocks the sparse lighting, shadows dance around the bones. Water drips and echoes in the distance, and sounds carry as they bounce around the limestone walls. The skulls certainly add to the very supernatural mood.

Near the end of your Catacomb tour, it's worth reminding yourself that these people all had names. Every one of them was a person. Those 6 million people sacrificed their eternal resting ground so the city of Paris could grow and thrive. Noblemen's bones are intertwined with peasants, families' skeletal remains may be crushed with their ancestors' bones, and visitors walk through all of it. There are 30 generations speaking to each passerby, forced into a single collective voice. If you listen closely, you may just hear some of those voices.

Chapter 9:
BIG NOSE KATE'S SALOON

Big Nose Kate's is a restaurant, gift shop, and saloon, in the heart of historic Tombstone, Arizona. Local ghost tours always make the bar a stop on their walks. Photo by Cody Polston.

BIG NOSE KATE'S SALOON:

Tombstone, Arizona

Tel: 1 (520) 457-3107

Web: *www.bignosekate.com*

The Old West is a place where legends were made and sometimes unmade, in towns and counties that were, at times, lawless. Miners rushed to gold and silver claims with hopes of striking it rich, or at least making enough to survive and dig another day. Tombstone, Arizona *is* the Old West. Right in the heart of this living relic of a town is Big Nose Kate's, a place that has witnessed the gunslingers; the miners; the ladies of the evening; and the life, death, and even the afterlife of the Old West.

Big Nose Kate's is now a saloon and restaurant, but it sits on the ruins of the famous Grand Hotel built in 1879. The Grand Hotel was the place to stay in Tombstone. It was the place the Clantons and the McLaurys stayed on October 25, 1881, the night before they would face "Doc" Holliday and Wyatt, Virgil, and Morgan Earp in the gunfight at the OK Corral.

So who was Big Nose Kate? Katherine Elder was the first prostitute in Tombstone, and she ran the first combination brothel and saloon in town. Kate was also the on-again, off-again girlfriend of Doc Holliday. After Kate helped him escape from jail in Fort Griffin, Texas, Holliday married Big Nose Kate, though he never made her a completely honest woman. Holliday never gave up gambling and gun slinging, and Kate never gave up her chosen profession—yet the couple stayed together in spite of their unconventional lifestyles.

Tombstone was a boomtown—the silver mines were yielding rich veins of the precious metal, and prospectors closed in on Tombstone from all over to work the mines. In 1881, Tombstone boasted a population of almost 5,000 people, 110 saloons, and 14 gambling halls.

When the Grand Hotel was in operation, there was an old miner everyone called "the Swamper." The Swamper was a janitor and general handyman for the hotel. He was an honest and trusted man, who did his work in exchange for a room, though certainly not one of the 16 carpeted and mahogany-furnished guest rooms that were for rent above ground. The Swamper's living quarters were in the dark basement of the hotel—and he wouldn't have been happier anywhere else. Today, the Swamper's room is still preserved next to Big Nose Kate's gift shop, and it looks more like a section of mineshaft than even a closet, let alone a bedroom. Dark wood beams support the walls, and a small, wrought iron-framed bed in the corner of the cramped space gives the only indication that someone would actually consider sleeping there.

The Swamper spent years digging a tunnel from the basement into one of the many shafts of the silver mines that ran under the town. Considering his housing expenses were covered by his labor, this strange, subterranean-dwelling man was able to hoard his silver nuggets for years. Some local lore says that the Swamper wasn't the only one using the new tunnel to the Grand Hotel basement. Allegedly, other miners would occasionally pop out of the hole to have a quick drink at the bar before going back to work.

Though the fruits of the Swamper's tunneling efforts to the mine shaft can still be seen today, in the basement of Big Nose Kate's saloon, no one is sure what became of his stock of silver.

The Swamper may still be dwelling in his basement to this day. Many ghost reports at the saloon are centered in the basement. Some of the locals say that if you utter the name "Swamper" in the basement of Big Nose Kate's, you'll feel the old-timer's presence emerge from his preserved room.

Tricia Rawson has been studying the ghosts and history of Tombstone since 1994. She said, "The first time I came to Tombstone, I just didn't understand why I personally was feeling so many spirits here—and so many spirits at unrest. I know that anywhere you had a boomtown back then, where everything was so lawless, you had a tremendous amount of sudden trauma deaths. But it was more than that.

It was very overwhelming to me, and I didn't understand why this area had so much energy going on."

Since 2003, Rawson has been conducting spirit walks in Tombstone and has spent plenty of her time in Big Nose Kate's. She said of their basement: "Some employees have been so scared downstairs that they won't go back down there. I know the gate downstairs going into the old, little hole there will literally open and stop right mid-frame and then close back again, as if someone came through and pushed it as far as they needed to and then pushed it closed. That happens all of the time down there."

Today, the main bar of Big Nose Kate's sits where the old lobby of the Grand Hotel used to be. The Grand Hotel did have a bar, but it was in the basement below the lobby. Kate's still runs a second bar in the downstairs, but the main action is at street-level. Stepping through Kate's bat-wing doors is like walking into the Old West again. Due to a town-wide fire in 1882, only two original bars survived. One now sits in the Bird Cage Theatre Museum, and the other is still in full operation at Big Nose Kate's. Saloon patrons can buy a drink at the very bar Wyatt Earp, Doc Holliday, and Ike Clanton ordered from more than a century ago.

It was at this historic bar that Rawson had a peculiar ghostly experience with one of her redheaded girlfriends. Rawson said, "One of my girlfriends was in there with me one night, and she sat on one of the bar stools and it started twirling on her. You could see the muscles in her legs pushing her feet up against the sidewall of the bar, trying to stay in position, and the stool was just spinning her around—not real fast, but it was a force that wasn't going to let her sit still. It ended up drawing a crowd, because it did it for almost 45 minutes. I said, 'Well, whoever it is really likes redheads.'"

Rawson believes there are many ghosts besides the Swamper who haunt the saloon. She said, "You just know when you go in there really early in the morning or really late at night when it's real quiet—you just know there's all kinds of [spirits of] people sitting there in the bar."

Unseen forces have toyed with Rawson all over Big Nose Kate's. "I've had them [ghosts] yank my hair back, touch me, walk by me when there's no one there," she said. "Chairs beside me move like someone just walked up and pulled out a chair to sit down."

Tim Ferrick, better known as "Whiskers" around Tombstone, has been the manager of Big Nose Kate's since 1996. His wife, Marcy, though the locals call her "Stormy"—the name her grandfather gave her—manages the attached Longhorn Restaurant. I got to speak with Stormy about the ghosts at Kate's. She said some of the more common occurrences include being pinched (especially the ladies), hearing boot steps on the dance floor, and lights that get turned on and off on their own.

Stormy and Whiskers were introduced to the ghosts of Big Nose Kate's in 1996 when they first spoke with the saloon's owners about employment. Stormy said, "We arrived at Tombstone in the late evening. The owner had closed the doors for the night, and we sat at a table at one corner of the saloon. About a half hour into our discussion, the owner began to talk about some of the ghostly legends at the saloon. Just then, a movement from the small balcony caught everyone's attention. On the balcony were two mannequins, a man and a woman dressed in 1800s-period clothing. We watched as the female mannequin, who was originally seated far behind the railing, moved to the railing, leaned over, and fell to the floor. We were stunned by the crash of the body. Then we saw the male mannequin's head quickly turn toward the direction where the female had been. We promptly got out of our chairs and called it a night after that!"

The next day, they examined the mannequins but couldn't find a reason why one would tumble over a railing. On another occasion, in the lower section of the saloon, Stormy felt she was getting a helping hand from a spirit she's taken to calling "Felix." Two intoxicated men came down to the basement gift shop where Stormy was working alone. She had a bad feeling these men might be up to trouble. "I figured I'd just call up security and have him pass through as a little deterrent kind of thing. But before I could do that, I felt a hand on my left shoulder. Where I was standing behind the bar, I could see both entrances—one that the employees would use and one that the customers would use. Nobody had come down the stairway, and it was just the three of us. The guys just looked at me, shocked, and said, 'We're out of here!' and then they quickly went back up the spiral staircase. The hand stayed on my shoulder until the men had vacated the area. The hand didn't bother me; in fact, when it touched my shoulder, it was more of a calming effect, like everything is going to be okay—nothing is going to happen." Stormy doesn't know what the drunken men saw behind her, but it was enough to send them scurrying up the stairs and out of the saloon.

Many a ghostly photo has been snapped at Big Nose Kate's Saloon, including a relatively famous photo of what looks like a semi-translucent horse at the bar, taken by local photojournalist Jim Kidd. We know the bar area has activity, and certainly the Swamper's basement does as well, but it turns out even the space in between is haunted. There are two staircases leading to the lower level—a spiral staircase in the center of the saloon and a wooden staircase at the back of the bar. Up until the late 1990s, there were many reports on the back staircase about women being pushed from behind when they were about three steps from the bottom of the staircase. This event seemed to be focused on women who walked down the stairs alone. Men and groups of people were left alone. In the late 1990s, the staircase was replaced and rebuilt, because it was falling apart from years of wear. After the rebuilding, the strange event of being pushed from behind stopped.

Cody Polston is the President of the Southwest Ghost Hunter's Association (SGHA) and has been researching the supernatural since the early 1980s. I spoke with Polston about his group's multiple investigations at the saloon. He said, "There's definitely something going on there." SGHA first investigated Kate's on September 2, 2000, after the bar had closed for the night. The group's methods are scientific—they bring devices to measure temperature, electromagnetic fields, and radiation. If ghostly phenomena are happening, they want to be able to take readings on all of the variables. Likewise, they want to be able to rule out natural effects. Their first visit yielded a few curious spikes on their equipment and some orbs and mists on their photos.

One year later, on September 2, 2001, Polston and SGHA were back again for their second formal investigation. This time, Polston witnessed something firsthand. He said, "I was talking to one of the bartenders, just chitchatting—not about ghosts or anything. They locked everything up and we were there late. We could hear a rattling down at the end of the bar, and out of the corner of my eye, a glass had come up off of the bar and just flew across the room. Of course it hit the ground and broke. I said, 'What was that?' Well, he [the bartender] reaches down, pulls out a list, and says, 'Damn, that's the fifth one this month.' I said, 'What are you doing?' He said, 'We have to keep track of the ones that get broken by the ghosts.'"

The Old West is still alive and well at Big Nose Kate's Saloon. The entire town of Tombstone is a reminder of the way people lived in the late 1800s, when laws were in the hands of lynch mobs, and you lived and died by the mine and by the gun. Some, such as Wyatt Earp and Doc Holliday, reached legend status, while others are buried in obscurity in nearby Boothill Graveyard. Today, the legends and the obscure still mingle in the cold spots, darting shadows, and ghostly manifestations of Tombstone.

Chapter 10:
Ordsall Hall

Ordsall Hall is a period house and local history museum. The hall is open to visitors Monday through Friday, 10 a.m. to 4 p.m., and Sunday, 1 p.m. to 4 p.m. It is closed Saturdays. Photo courtesy of Ordsall Hall.

ORDSALL HALL:

Salford, England

Tel: 44 (0) 161-872-0251

Web: *www.salford.gov.uk/ordsallhall*

Here lies Lord have mercy upon her;
One of Elizabeth's maids of honour.
Margaret Radclyffe fair and witty;
She died a maid, the more the pity.

Margaret Radclyffe's gravestone is inscribed with the preceding epitaph. Radclyffe died November 10, 1599 at the age of 25. She was one of Queen Elizabeth's maids of honor, one of the top six ladies in the royal court. The young maiden died in the building she grew up and lived in: Ordsall Hall. Because of her royal connections, she would receive a semi-state funeral and be interred in Westminster Abbey in London, but her spirit will always be at Ordsall Hall.

Located outside the northwestern English city of Manchester, we know some sort of structure was built in 1177 C.E. where Ordsall Hall is now, because the name "Ordeshala" appears to have paid a feudal tax in the old public records of that year. In 1335, though, the manor house passed into the Radclyffe family, where the building would be expanded, as would the Radclyffe family's numbers.

The Radclyffes were a prestigious family in England. Many were knighted for their valor in battles in wars, such as the English Civil War, and in battles against the Spanish Armada and against the Scottish revolt in the north.

The focus of most of Ordsall Hall's ghostly activity can be traced to Margaret Radclyffe, who was born in either 1573 or 1574—though her death date is known with certainty, her exact birth date is not. Margaret had a twin brother named Alexander, whom she was very close to her whole life. Both siblings were in the court of Queen Elizabeth and certainly had more than their share of political clout. Along with the prestige also came a sense of duty. In 1599, Alexander joined the Earl of Essex and Queen Elizabeth's troops in Ireland, to fight the Irish rebels who were uprising against the Queen's appointment of Essex as Lord Lieutenant of Ireland. The battle would be the greatest offensive launched abroad by Queen Elizabeth, and it would be a war from which Alexander Radclyffe would not return. When news of her dear brother's death reached Margaret, she was literally heartbroken.

Young Margaret Radclyffe died just a few weeks after her brother did. The official cause of death was "strings around the heart," which today we know as angina brought on by stress. The legend says Margaret Radclyffe is forever waiting for her brother to return from Ireland, and she won't go until he does.

The ghost legends of Ordsall Hall do seem to point to the possibility of several ghosts—at least one inside is assumed to be that of Margaret Radclyffe, and the other, a "white lady" who roams the grounds around the hall. This may also be Margaret, but folklore has a second and third suspect.

Harrison Ainsworth's 1840 novel, *The Gunpowder Treason: An Historical Romance*, made Ordsall Hall the setting of the famous Gunpowder Plot, where Guy Fawkes and Robert Catesby planned to overthrow King James. Ainsworth's tale has Fawkes in a passionate love affair with Viviana Radclyffe before heading off to try and blow up the House of Parliament in 1605. Though a lot of Ainsworth's novel is based on history, no record of a Viviana Radclyffe can be found. However, the fiction and folklore have mixed enough that the street adjacent to the Hall has been called "Guy Fawkes Street," and there is an annual festival at Ordsall Hall in Fawkes' honor.

Some people have said that the "white lady" of Ordsall Hall is that of Viviana Radclyffe; however, the history isn't there to support putting this name to the ghost who walks the grounds.

There is also a third legend of whom the white lady was. Some say she was a jilted bride-to-be who was left standing at the altar of

Saint Cyprian's Church, which once stood next to Ordsall Hall. The grief-stricken girl was reported to have climbed the stairs in the Great Hall and thrown herself out of an open window to her death. The building is not very tall—only three stories at its tallest window. It's questionable whether the leap would be enough to kill a person. Yet, one thing is for certain: there is some peculiar pale female figure walking around the grounds of Ordsall Hall.

I spoke with Les Willis, a life-long Salfordian and a senior enabler, or guide, at the Hall. He's been working at Ordsall Hall since 1992. Willis told me about the previous supervisor who was living at the Hall with his wife when they received a call in the middle of the night from the home for the elderly, across the street. Willis said, "It was 3:00 in the morning when this telephone call came asking, 'What's your wife doing outside walking around on the grounds?' And he said, 'She's actually sleeping next to me.' Somebody from the elderly people's home had actually spotted some white shape and thought it was the supervisor's wife."

This wasn't the first report of a white lady outside. Willis said he remembers hearing the ghostly legends when he was a child in Salford.

The Radclyffes lived in Ordsall Hall for more than 300 years. By the end of the 17th century, the home would pass among other families as their private residence and eventually be turned into a working men's club, church hall, antique shop, theological training center, and since April 1972, the hall has been a period house and local history museum owned and operated by the city of Salford. In its entire history, Ordsall Hall has never sat empty.

Today there is no longer a moat or acres of forest surrounding the hall. It is now set rather peculiarly in between a 1970s housing estate and an industrial estate. The Tudor-style, half-timbered, black-and-white manor is, itself, an artifact of history—the only half-timbered Tudor left in the region. Walking into the museum is like walking into a warm and friendly 17th-century home, right down to the furnishings.

The museum receives as many as 20,000 visitors per year, many of whom are schoolchildren who come to dress in Elizabethan era costumes and learn something about their local history.

In the 12 years Les Willis has been working at the hall, he has heard many reports of strange cold spots, especially in the Star Chamber, which is the oldest section of the building. But ghostly encounters are not confined to just the Star Chamber. In the adjoining Great Hall, many people have experienced the supernatural either in person or from anywhere in the world via the Ordsall Hall "Ghost Cam." Many ghost hunters on the Web may remember the Ordsall Hall Web camera, mounted in the Great Hall and streaming constant video surveillance of the room to the Web. There are many strange pictures that were captured on the Web cam, from round orbs to a pale gray apparition on the staircase in the big room.

Willis has experienced doors closing behind him when there was no wind or person to push it, and he's seen a lot of electrical and camera equipment fail—especially in the Star Chamber. Willis said, "I've got a friend who takes pictures of the building with a digital camera. All of his pictures turn out in color, and just one room [the Star Chamber] turns out in black and white. That happened two days running; he came back and took the same photographs the following day, and it went into black and white. We've also had television companies come who've set up lots of cameras, they've blown, and it shouldn't have happen. Things like that we can't explain. Maybe they got a surge through the electrics or something like that. So maybe they get a surge to the electrics that did major damage to their expensive lights but doesn't hurt our CD player."

The strange electrical surges are regular occurrences at Ordsall Hall. But blowing out lighting rigs isn't the only prank the ghostly residents like to play. Around the Hall, but especially in the Star Chamber, staff members have reported simple items, such as keys, going missing. Then they'll turn up days or weeks later in a completely different place. The Star Chamber is also home to another phenomena that assaults a different sense. Denise Roberts has been working at Ordsall Hall since 2001, and she has encountered a powerful scent in the Star Chamber. Roberts said, "Occasionally we get smells in that room. It smells like dead bodies. Like dirty, dirty people. Like somebody who hasn't washed for a long, long time. It smells like several dirty people have all wandered into the room at the same time, and the smell will come and go very quickly. It might stay for 10 minutes and then it goes, but with no sign of where it's gone to."

The most profound encounter that Willis experienced happened during a break with one of his colleagues. He said, "We were off downstairs and I had just noticed, through the corner of my eye, something going up the stairs—and we could hear footsteps. We both heard the same thing."

Ordsall Hall has had its ghostly residents even in modern times. Willis told me of two local women who lived in the hall as children, when their father was the caretaker. In the summer of 2003, these two women paid a visit to Ordsall Hall for the first time since they had moved out. Willis recounted the story that one of the elderly women told him: "She said she had a young play friend here. The play friend was Valerie; she [was an imaginary friend]. And being a child, she couldn't work out 'Valerie,' because V's are very hard for young children, so she used to call her 'Celery.'"

Roberts continued the story. She said, "They told us that they regularly had encounters with a small girl in Elizabethan costume who called herself Valerie. She actually used to speak to them. When they came back here after all of those years, strange things happened. They were going down one flight of stairs, and then all of a sudden one of the sisters said to the other sister that she could feel Valerie around her. As soon as she said that, one of the light fixtures came crashing to the floor, breaking into quite a few pieces—dead on cue, it seemed. The women both looked at each other and said 'That was Valerie.' That she was trying to make her presence felt to them. Then they went into the great hall, and they called me in and told me to stand in this corner, and they said, 'What can you smell?' And I could smell roses and I could smell lavender—I could smell all sorts of sweet-scented flowers. But there were no flowers in the room. And they said, 'That's Valerie, and she's standing with us.'"

Roberts explained how one particular part of the building produces a lot of strange noises, like furniture being moved and banging sounds. The two women believed they knew what was happening. Roberts said, "It's one of the places that they said Valerie used to play. They reckoned that that's Valerie."

During their summer visit, the two women could no longer see their ghostly childhood friend, Valerie, but they knew she was still there. Roberts said, "When they were children, they used to see her, so maybe you lose something growing older, because they couldn't see her anymore."

Sam Smith is the museum supervisor for Ordsall Hall; she's worked there since 1998. She told me her take on the hall: "It's one of those buildings where you often have the feeling that there's somebody behind you. But there isn't," Smith said. "There have been several times where I've heard the office door open and I've got up to go see who it is, but the door's shut and there's nobody there. It just sticks in my mind because you have to open the door with a key. So it's hearing that lock turn, but there's nothing there."

The office resides in the newest part of the building, the section constructed in the 1600s. Smith has also experienced the uneasy feeling of sensing a person standing behind her in one of the oldest parts of the building. In the East Wing is the Solar Room, a chamber not open to the public. Smith claims that, when standing by the room's fireplace, she gets the feeling someone is there with her, even though her eyes verify she's in the room alone.

Willis said, "We surely should have a ghost if we've been around for 800 years. If we haven't got a ghost in 800 years, then I think we're doing something wrong. We receive something like 10,000 school-children a year as visitors—and they're not quiet, and we don't want them to be quiet. If that doesn't get rid of the ghosts, nothing will."

Ordsall Hall allows its visitors to step back to the Elizabethan age in a welcoming and very historic Tudor home. With all of the children and company, it's no wonder Margaret Radclyffe feels compelled to stay and entertain her guests while she waits for her fallen brother to return.

Chapter 11:
THE WHITE HOUSE

Tours of the State Floor of the White House are available, though you should check the White House Website or call for details on arranging a tour in advance. Photo by Philip Greenspun, *philip.greenspun.com*.

THE WHITE HOUSE:

Washington, D.C.

Tel: 1 (202) 456-7041

Web: *www.whitehouse.gov*

TOP SECRET

In school, I learned how the different branches of government operate, and the teachers covered some history of the early construction projects in Washington, but they didn't tell us about the ghosts. Without a doubt, 1600 Pennsylvania Avenue is one of the most famous addresses in the United States. The White House is home to some real American spirits—a former president and first lady—and even a British soldier still lost and confused from the War of 1812.

The perils of running a nation at war with itself and, at times, other countries and struggling with all the internal issues of economy, health, and education of this relatively young nation have weighed heavily on the minds and hearts of presidents, members of their families, and their administrations. Ghost sightings in the White House are a regular occurrence to this day. Even skeptics (or those officials who would never admit they believe in ghosts for fear of political repercussions) feel something strange there. White House Chief Usher Gary Walters, who has served every president since Richard Nixon, said in a Halloween 2003 online chat, "The presidents who I have worked for have all indicated a feeling of the previous occupants of the White House and have all talked about drawing strength from the fact that the previous presidents have lived here."

During the Constitutional Convention of 1787, the nation's forefathers decided it was important to build a strong central government.

General George Washington was to oversee the designing and building of the young nation's capital that would be, per Article I, Section 8 of the Constitution, "not exceeding ten miles square," on the Potomac River. At the center of the new city would be the president's home.

A national competition was held to select a design for this important building, and James Hoban's design for a Georgian-style mansion prevailed. In 1792, construction began of "the people's house." The workers were comprised mostly of slaves, on loan from local plantations, and skilled immigrant workers.

The stone walls were built 4 feet thick, with ornate adornments around the windows and on its whitewashed stone façade. The original building contained 64 rooms on three levels but had no indoor plumbing and only fireplaces for heat. President Washington died in 1799 and never lived to see the completion of the great house. President John Adams and his wife Abigail would be the first to spend the night in the newly constructed home for the president on November 1, 1800.

Photo courtesy of the Library of Congress.

Less than 14 years later, the new building was almost lost forever. In August of 1814, the British invaded Washington, D.C., during the War of 1812. At the time, President James Madison was in office and was expecting 40 guests for a dinner that his wife, Dolley, had spent most of the day preparing. When it became evident that the city was on the verge of being sacked, the president and first lady narrowly escaped with their lives, the Gilbert Stuart portrait of

George Washington, and a precious few other belongings before British soldiers stormed the White House, ate the food Dolley Madison had prepared, and then set fire to the president's home. Though the exact British death toll on the D.C. raid is uncertain, there have been reports over the years of a ghost of a lost British soldier carrying a torch.

After the fire, all that remained were the four stone walls of the house. Everything inside was reduced to ashes. There was talk of moving the nation's capital inland, to avoid future military risk, but President Madison insisted on rebuilding. The house was indeed rebuilt, cleaned, and brought back better than before. The outside walls were whitewashed with paint again, save for two spots. Near the North Portico and on what was to eventually be called the Truman Balcony, there are still sections that show the burn marks of 1814. They serve as a reminder of what happened almost two centuries ago.

Arguably the most troubled presidency in the history of the president's mansion was Abraham Lincoln's. Inaugurated on March 4, 1861, America's 16th president faced a nation torn in two by the Civil War. Lincoln made the decision to reunite the Union, by force if necessary—and the force necessary to accomplish this great task was about as much as Lincoln's spirit could bear. Brother against brother, parent against child, tens of thousands of citizens would lose their lives to the Civil War, which began at Fort Sumter on April 12, 1861.

Lincoln felt personally responsible for the deaths of so many, and one of his few areas of reprieve from the burden of leading a nation at war with itself was his family. When Lincoln's son, William Wallace Lincoln, died of a typhoid-like disease in the White House on February 20, 1862, Lincoln's heart broke. Young Willy was the favorite son of Abraham and Mary Todd Lincoln. A handsome, intelligent, mature-for-his-age, and quick-witted child, all who encountered him in the White House remembered the striking lad. William's ghost was the first reported supernatural encounter in the White House.

As quoted in an online article, "William Wallace Lincoln (1850-1862)," by The Lincoln Institute, Katherine Helm recounts Mary Todd Lincoln's experience as communicated to her half-sister, Emilie Todd Helm:

> "He comes to me every night, and stands at the foot of my bed with the same sweet, adorable smile he has always had; he does not always come alone; little Eddie [Lincoln's second

son, who died at age 3] is sometimes with him and twice he has come with our brother Alec, he tells me he loves his Uncle Alec and is with him most of the time. You cannot dream of the comfort this gives me. When I thought of my little son in immensity, alone, without his mother to direct him, no one to hold his little hand in loving guidance, it nearly broke my heart."

Abraham Lincoln was elected to a second term but would never live to see it through. John Wilkes Booth's bullet found its mark on Lincoln at the Ford Theatre on April 15, 1865. Lincoln would be the second president to lie in state in the White House's East Room. There would be five more presidents to receive the same funeral honors before the end of the 20th century.

Mary Todd may not have been the last to feel the presence of her son in the White House. In his memoir, *Taft and Roosevelt: The Intimate Letters of Archie Butt, Military Aide*, Archibald Butt, in a letter to Clara Butt dated July 26, 1911, said:

"It seems that the White House is haunted. This was a most interesting piece of news to me, for it seemed to me to be the only thing wanting to make the White House the most interesting spot in the United States. The ghost, it seems, is a young boy from its description.... The housekeeper, a spooky little person herself, informs me that he has been felt more often than he has been seen, but when I remonstrated with her that ghosts have not the sense of touch, at least those self-respecting ghosts of which I have heard, she insisted that it was this manifestation of the Thing which caused such fright among the servants."

During the first half of the 1900s, the White House was starting to be noticeably insufficient quarters for the president's home, office, and increasingly, his world stage. In 1901, Theodore Roosevelt would add on the West Wing to house the new Oval Office and free up room in the main mansion. Rooms such as Lincoln's presidential office were converted to bedrooms and other living quarters.

In 1920, a new floor, built of modern concrete and steel, was added to the top of the building to provide more space for living quarters. Unfortunately, though the new space was sturdy, it was also too heavy for the old wooden construction underneath it. Several different presidents, staff, and guests heard noises, sometimes described as footsteps in the White House. Skeptics attributed the sounds to the old house creaking. But while sounds are one thing, physical manifestations are another.

During Woodrow Wilson's presidency (1913–1921), First Lady Ellen Louise Axson ordered Dolley Madison's beloved rose garden to be removed. According to White House folklore, when the garden staff walked up to the rose garden with spades and picks in hand, they encountered the angry specter of Dolley Madison. The rose garden still stands to this day and has served as the backdrop for many Presidential press conferences.

In 1941, Queen Wilhelmina of the Netherlands paid a visit to the White House and stayed as a guest of President Franklin Roosevelt and First Lady Eleanor Roosevelt. While sleeping in the Lincoln Bedroom, the Queen reportedly heard knocking at her door. When she opened the door, she encountered the ghost of Abraham Lincoln staring back at her from the hallway.

In 1948, President Harry Truman began a four-year restoration project. The White House was completely gutted, and the interior stone walls were replaced with steel beam construction. Modern air conditioning, electrical conduits, and plumbing were also added, and two additional floors were built underground. The mansion grew to 132 rooms, with the main house being used for entertaining, formal meetings, and living quarters, and offices being located in the wings of the White House.

The updates did not scare the ghosts away by any means. More reports of sightings and other strange occurrences continue even to this day. Tony Savoy, White House operations foreman, discussed his encounter with the ghost of President Lincoln in an interview on the official White House Website: "It was early one morning, and I was taking care of the plants up on the second floor.... When I turned the light on one morning, he was sitting there outside his office with his hands over top of each other, legs crossed, and was looking straight ahead. He had a gray, charcoal [colored] pin-striped suit on, and he had a pair of three-button spats turned over on the side with black shoes on. He was sitting there, and he startled me and I stopped. And when I blinked, he was gone. And I left there and went down the stairs and told assistant usher Nelson Pierce what I had seen. And he said I'm just one of the other ones that had seen him throughout the house over the past years."

Dennis Freemyer, White House assistant usher, said of his encounter, "I've been here almost 25 years. I've only had one experience upstairs, and it was back during the Reagan administration. Normally we have a gentleman that works here in the evenings that turns out all the lights at the first family's request and kind of shuts the place down for the night, and he was out sick that night so I was doing his job. I'd gone upstairs and turned out lights in a number of rooms. I went to the Lincoln Bedroom, and there's a chandelier there that had a light switch that was a dimmer-type that you just push in and it turns it off—a rheostat. So I turned that light off, turned out some other lights, went into a series of other rooms, went across the hallway into what's called the Queen's Bedroom, and as I came out of the Queen's Bedroom, I was looking directly into a darkened Lincoln Bedroom, and all of a sudden the chandelier came back on.

"Of course I'd been aware of some of the stories and all, so I ran in right away, hoping that I'd get to see something or feel something and really didn't see anything at first. I turned off the chandelier, and then I got a very cold chill. I could definitely feel something, so I kind of looked around. I looked in the mirror thinking maybe there was something behind me, which of course there wasn't. But without a doubt, I could feel a very cold presence of someone/something there."

The Lincoln Bedroom has certainly been a hot spot for supernatural occurrences in the White House. On the History Channel's *The White House: 200th Anniversary*, former First Lady Rosalynn Carter said of the infamous room, "They were so overwhelmed by being in that place.... Most of our friends who spent the night in the Lincoln Bedroom didn't sleep."

White House chief usher Gary Walters described his encounter that occurred near a staircase between the East Room and North Portico. There are two large doors that are secured to their walls in an open position. Walters said, "These doors are open 24 hours a day, never locked, and in the open position without being closed. There were three of us standing here in the vicinity of these doors, and we felt a cold rush of air pass through us. It seemed like it came from the staircase and from these doors. The doors, after we felt the cold rush of air, came slowly closed—something that none of us had ever seen before, and we proceeded to the North Portico doors and looked to see if maybe somebody had opened the doors and created a vacuum, or possibly if somebody had opened a door downstairs.

We looked in both areas and didn't find any explanation for why these doors that are open on a 24-hour-a-day circumstance would all of a sudden close. That's one of the mysteries of the White House, and some people wonder if that may have been Lincoln's ghost that went through."

All around the White House there are reminders of past presidents and of more than 200 years of American history. From the furniture to the paintings, each president has made some impression on this mansion. Decisions about wars, economic struggles, and family turmoil have wrestled with the hearts and minds of every American president. Some great triumphs and great tragedies have been seen and felt at this historic building as the rest of us looked on. There is no doubt that some of the nation's forefathers are still concerned and still paying close attention to the country and building they gave so much of themselves to.

Chapter 12:
THE ALASKAN HOTEL

The hotel does not give tours; however, its lobby and bar room are open to the public. Photo by Jeff Belanger.

THE ALASKAN HOTEL:

Juneau, Alaska

Tel: 1 (800) 327-9347

Web: *www.ptialaska.net/~akhotel/index.html*

"We followed the gulch down from the summit of the mountain into the basin...and it was a beautiful sight to see the large pieces of quartz spangled over with gold," Richard Harris said on October 3, 1880, according to Nancy Warren Ferrell's online article, "The Founding of Juneau, Alaska." On that momentous day, Joe Juneau and Richard Harris, along with their Tlingit Indian guide, found gold in Silver Bow Basin, in a stream they called Gold Creek. This event ignited a nationwide gold rush to this largely untapped section of the world. Over the years, many people came to the wilds of Alaska searching for this precious metal. But there's more than just gold to be found—there are ghosts in those hills and towns, too.

A trip up Alaska's southeastern coast will bring you through a natural channel of islands and inlets known as the Inside Passage. En route from Canada's southwestern border with the Pacific Ocean up to Alaska's capital of Anchorage, you'll pass through towns such as Ketchikan, Wrangell, Sitka, Juneau, Skagway, Haines, and Valdez. The only way to reach these towns is by boat or plane—roads and rails can't connect with these secluded communities because of glacier-filled bordering mountains and extremely rugged terrain.

The history of these Alaskan towns is colorful but fraught with danger. Some early gold rushers found their fortune, others sought riches their entire, short lives but only made enough money to survive for another day of digging—gold fever drove them onward desperately trying to find the mother lode. Gold fever could be so infectious that one could forget time itself.

Alaska was a Russian territory until it was sold to the United States in 1867. Prior to the sale, Russia's main interest in Alaska was sea otter pelts and other fur-trading activities—very few had explored the possibility of finding gold in any great quantity. After the United States purchased Alaska and raised its flag over Castle Hill in the former Russian capital of Sitka, some prospectors caught word that conditions may be right to find gold—and lots of it. These men wandered up the coast to Alaska to seek their fortune.

After Harris and Juneau's golden discovery in 1880, the Alaskan gold rush was on in full force. These coastal Alaskan towns got their start as simple tent villages, where miners slept when they weren't digging or panning for gold. Eventually, buildings were erected, saloons opened, hotels and general stores began to take shape, and these campsites turned into towns.

Alaska offers nature in all of its power and glory, but it can also offer its visitors many ghostly legends. In the state capital of Juneau—a city of approximately 31,000 people—there is a particularly "lively" haunting. On a quaint street called South Franklin, in the heart of downtown Juneau, sits the Alaskan Hotel.

The Alaskan Hotel is a three-story, grey, stone-faced building with decorative red, white, and blue wood delineating the stories of the 46-room hotel. The Canadian, U.S., and state flags wave proudly above the sidewalk in front. The first floor is home to the small lobby and front office, but most of the floor is taken up by the attached bar. The pub features the local ales on tap, and fine woodwork with a rich, deep stain surrounds the bar as well as the doors, stage, and ceiling molding. The hotel has been preserved in its original Victorian style and looks similar to the way it must have looked almost a century ago. The Alaskan also has the distinction of being on the national register of historic places.

The Alaskan Hotel was built in 1913 by brothers James and John McCloskey and entrepreneur Jules B. Caro. After striking it rich northeast of Juneau, the McCloskeys acquired prime real estate—close to the steamship docks, and in the heart of the business district. Jules Caro brought the idea and additional capital needed to build a hotel. Construction began in March of 1913 and was completed in time for a September 16 opening. The management sent out invitations for the gala event which said, "At 6 p.m. the management will formally unlock the doors and the keys will then be attached to a toy balloon which will carry them out of sight. From the moment the doors swing open, never to close, the hotel will be for the accommodation of guests."

The Alaskan Hotel is Juneau's oldest continuously operating hotel. Originally a hotel and bordello, the establishment was set up for miners who were camped in town while they sought their fortune in the surrounding streams and mountains. The Alaskan Hotel offered these men a place to play and a place to spend some of the gold they worked so hard to find.

In the late 1800s and early 1900s, the men significantly outnumbered the women in Alaska. Houses of prostitution were popular places to be when the men weren't working. According to Ron Wendt, author of *Haunted Alaska*, a collection of ghost stories from America's last frontier, the ghost that haunts the Alaskan Hotel is that of a woman who was driven to become a prostitute when her husband had gone into the hills to mine for three weeks and didn't return. She ran out of money and thought that maybe her husband wasn't coming back at all, so she became a lady of the night. Three weeks later, her husband did return and was so angry when he found out what she was doing that he killed her in the hotel.

The locals have more than one legend about how the haunting started. After speaking with several people who worked at the hotel, some patrons, and even a former manager, it is clear that not everyone agrees on which part of the hotel has the most activity or how the haunting got started, but they do all agree it is haunted. It seems all of the locals know of the Alaskan Hotel's ghostly residents.

Jake Good, who works at the front desk of the hotel said, "People have told me they've seen things before, like seeing people in the hallways that look like people in paintings around here. I've never experienced any of that kind of stuff, but I've heard about it. The only reason that I personally believe that it's haunted around here is because parts of the hotel just don't feel right. Some parts of the hotel I just don't feel safe at—I'm constantly turning around."

Good went on to talk about room 219 in the hotel. He said, "Whenever I walk up into room 219, I get goosebumps. It's cold in there all of the time for some reason. I personally think there are probably a couple of ghosts around here. I think the one in 219 is the only one that is frustrated or unhappy or tormented, I don't know."

Good has only been working at the Alaskan Hotel since the summer of 2003, but he said guests continually ask to be moved out of room 219. The patrons don't usually give much of a reason, and Good says he doesn't ask too many questions—he simply tries to accommodate them.

Scott Fry, a local musician, was the manager of the Alaskan Hotel for 12 years. Fry said, "Her name is Alice, if I remember correctly, and she supposedly was a lady of the night. She got killed, and I was told originally it was somewhere in the back of the building. She lost her life to a jealous lover."

Fry also spoke of specific rooms with ghostly activity. He said, "Room 218. I used to get people saying, 'She's in my room.' I've had people tell me that she was touching them, or they could see her sitting on the bed. A friend of mine told me if you walk up the top of the stairs, you could see her in the mirror by [room] 308. I've also had people tell me she was in the bar coming down the stairs. The bar has a lot of mirrors in it, and it's easy to see things out of the corner of your eye, especially if you're tired."

Fry said he has heard of activity in almost all of the rooms on the south side of the hotel. He himself never had any supernatural experiences in the Alaskan Hotel, but he has certainly heard many firsthand accounts from people who did.

Dan Ward has worked at the Alaskan Hotel off and on since 1974. He leaves once in a while to go down south to see family, and then he comes back to Juneau to work. Ward recalls when the present owners began restoring the hotel to its original Victorian style back in 1978, something he says has been ongoing in some form ever since.

Ward has never personally experienced anything supernatural, but he recounted some ghost stories he's heard from some of the staff at the Alaskan Hotel. He said, "Housekeepers used to always say there's one particular room where things would get moved around. They'd put towels someplace and come back 5 minutes later and they'd be somewhere else. I actually had a desk clerk one time who had just started—he was working the graveyard shift. He was sitting at the desk reading a book and you know how you kind of sense somebody walking up to you? He did that, and he looked up and he just got this image of a blond girl in a white dress. But when he actually got his head up there, there was nobody there."

Ron Wendt relayed a story he had heard from Elva Bontrager, who stayed in the Alaskan Hotel several years ago. Wendt said, "It wasn't long after she started working in Juneau that she started going to the Alaskan Hotel. She went into the bathroom there—it was an old-style bathroom—and then she came back out. The next time she went in, it was brand-new and she says, 'What happened to the old bathroom?' Everything had changed. It's a pretty tremendous thing when the whole room changes while you're there. She said others had also experienced that."

The people who live on the state's southeastern coast, in towns where everyone knows everyone else, have some intriguing stories and folklore to share. You may not find any precious metals in the streams and hills of Alaska, but you can find gold in the ghost stories of the great people who live there.

Chapter 13:
MONTE CRISTO HOMESTEAD

Notice the strange reflection of what looks like a woman in a black and white dress in the lower-left window? Monte Cristo Homestead is open 10 a.m. to 4 p.m. every day of the year except Christmas. Additionally, the Homestead museum allows overnight ghost tours by special arrangement. Contact them for details. Photo by Matt Bowden.

MONTE CRISTO HOMESTEAD:

Junee, New South Wales

Tel: 61 (02) 6924-1637

Web: *www.montecristo.com.au*

Monte Cristo literally means "Mount of Christ," but names and intentions can be deceiving. The late Victorian-era mansion, built in 1884, sits high on the hill overlooking the New South Wales town of Junee in Australia. The estate was the financial and social center of Christopher William Crawley's empire. Monte Cristo's grand stature and religious name are contrasted with the several untimely deaths, accidents, and acts of cruelty that would plague the homestead and lead to countless stories of tormented spirits who still walk the house and grounds today.

Crawley had acquired two parcels of land, totaling 520 acres, in January 1876, under provisions of Australia's Robertson Act of 1861. He struggled to farm his land and eke out a living, when a stroke of luck came his way. The Great Southern Railway Line was coming through and, moving on a tip, Crawley built the Railway Hotel across the road from what would soon become a busy rail station. With the rail in place, Crawley's ability to trade his agricultural products increased, as did his hotel business with the influx of travelers. The tiny village grew and Crawley bought more land with his mounting wealth. He would go on to be one of the town founders in 1883.

In 1876, Crawley built a small brick cottage for his family that is still standing today on the Monte Cristo property as the original homestead. In only eight years, the cottage no longer suited the

Crawleys' social status, and a new, grander edifice was needed. In 1884, a brick mansion was constructed of the finest materials. The old homestead became servants' quarters, stables were added for Mr. Crawley's prized horses, and a dairy building was constructed, as well as other out buildings on the property.

Mr. and Mrs. Crawley, their four daughters, and their three sons were the quintessential Victorian family—they dressed and acted in only the most fashionable manner and had the best of schooling. However, stories would surface years after they passed away of the unkind manner in which they ruled their estate.

In 1898, Mr. Crawley sold one of his properties, Junee's Loftus Hotel, for the giant sum of £10,000 to a Mrs. O'Donnald. Not trusting bank notes, Crawley insisted that the payment be made in gold sovereigns. The gold was delivered in a large sack, and Mr. Crawley counted the coins to make sure he wasn't short-changed before he signed over the deed to the hotel. There is no record of where the sovereigns went. Many believe the gold was hidden within the house or buried on the property. This bit of folklore would cause great troubles for Monte Cristo in its future.

The first official death at Monte Cristo occurred when one of the Crawleys' maids was carrying their infant daughter—the maid claimed an invisible force pushed the baby from her arms. The child went tumbling down the main staircase of the house and died from the trauma of the fall.

Mr. Crawley died at Monte Cristo on December 14, 1910, at the age of 69. He had developed a carbuncle on his neck—the infection was aggravated by his starched shirt collars—and disease spread to his bloodstream, causing heart failure. Mrs. Elizabeth Lydia Crawley was so distraught by the death of her husband that she became a shut-in. Much of the alleged cruelty stems from Mrs. Crawley, who lived many years beyond her husband. Additionally, the townspeople didn't respect Elizabeth without her husband around, due in part to racism; Elizabeth's part aboriginal lineage caused some of the locals to look down upon her mixed heritage. She converted one of the mansion's upstairs storage rooms into a chapel where she immersed herself in reading the Bible. Elizabeth hardly ventured off Monte Cristo for the last 23 years of her life, which ended August 12, 1933, due to a ruptured appendix.

Reginald Ryan has owned the Monte Cristo since 1963 and is an expert on the home's history. He told me about the cruelty that went on at Monte Cristo. He said, "There was a girl pushed off the balcony [though it was ruled as an accident]. She was a maid and was pregnant at the time, and she died. One of the young boys that was working and boarding here didn't get up for work one morning, and the boss said, 'Come to work,' and the boy said he was too sick. The boss thought he was acting and set fire to the straw mattress, and the boy didn't get out in time and was burned to death. The housekeeper's son was a mentally retarded chap named Harold Steele who was chained up in one of the out buildings for 40 years."

Harold Steele's story is perhaps the most heart-wrenching of all the Monte Cristo tragedies. In the estate's dairy building, poor Harold was chained to the wall like an animal. There is still a hole worn in the wall by his chain near the door. After Mrs. Crawley's death, Harold's mother assumed the role of caretaker of the home, and she and her son were the only full-time residents left at Monte Cristo. Sadly, Mrs. Steele died of a heart attack inside the main house, and it would be several days before anyone in town noticed they hadn't seen her. When the police finally investigated, they found Harold curled up in a fetal position, laying in his own filth. He was dehydrated, almost starved, and missing his mother terribly. Harold was turned over to Kenmore, a home for the mentally insane, where he died a few months later.

After Mrs. Steele's death, the house continued to deteriorate due to lack of upkeep. The last Crawley to live in the mansion vacated in 1948 leaving the estate vacant except for caretaker Jack Simpson. In 1961 the Hitchcock movie thriller *Psycho* came to Junee. After a local man saw the movie three times, he snapped, stalked up to Monte Cristo, and shot and killed the unsuspecting caretaker. Today, you can still see where either the murderer or some local with a morbid sense of humor carved "DIE JACK HA HA," into the door of the dairy building.

For the next two years, the house was completely open for vandals and looters who searched for Crawley's gold sovereigns and damaged the buildings.

The house held a lot of fascination with Wagga Wagga native, Reginald Ryan. In 1963, he and his wife, Olive, bought the homestead for £1,000. There were no windows left in the home, no electricity hook-up had ever been established, and vandals had damaged every room. But the Ryans had a dream of fixing it up and establishing an antiques business in the building.

Their first ghost experience happened just three days after moving in. Ryan said, "We had gone downtown in the evening to get some supplies, and as we drove back to the house, there was light streaming from every doorway and window. You know how lights go streaming out in a fog? Well, it was like that. And my wife was with me, so it wasn't just my imagination. We actually stopped the car and looked up at the house, and my wife wasn't particularly keen on coming up. But as we drove closer to the house, all the lights disappeared."

According to Ryan, there are at least 10 ghosts haunting Monte Cristo. Some psychics who visited the estate in the late 1990s for an Australian television show felt a woman who was murdered in the house was among the 10. Though no records of a murdered woman have been found there, it is possible that if something did happen, the Crawleys were held in such high regard that the local police probably wouldn't have asked too many questions.

Matt Bowden of the Australian Ghost Hunters Society (AGHS) is based in Australia's capital of Canberra. He first visited Monte Cristo looking for the supernatural in 2001, when he attended a ghost tour hosted by Reg Ryan. He told me about one peculiar incident in the mansion. Bowden said, "I experienced a few cold spots—especially in a room called the Drawing Room, where the lady of the house, Mrs. Crawley, would sit and sew. I experienced a cold spot in the corner of that room. At the time, there was a psychic on our tour, and she informed me that Mrs. Crawley was sitting in a chair next to where I was standing. I didn't see it, I couldn't exactly feel her presence as such, but I certainly felt a definite cold spot. I actually had a digital thermometer with me at the time—a piece of my ghost hunting equipment—and there certainly was a drop in temperature when I looked at the reading."

Bowden is quick to mention that, even though Monte Cristo has a gruesome past, which he was well aware of before ever stepping foot on the property, the home now has quite a warm and inviting feel to it.

In 2003, Bowden returned to Monte Cristo for a weekend stay with seven of his colleagues from AGHS. During the group's investigation, one of the psychically sensitive women in the group fell short of breath in the "Boys' Room" upstairs. Other psychics and mediums have also reported a heavy pressure on them in that room. The psychic from AGHS had to leave the room after a short period because of the pressure she felt on her chest.

In the upstairs Sitting Room, AGHS conducted a séance, to try and connect with the spirits of Monte Cristo. Bowden said, "I had done séances as a kid, but this one to me seemed very real. The planchette on the Ouija board was going crazy; it was just shooting all over the place, pointing everywhere. We got in touch with a guy called 'James.' He wasn't actually attached to the house, I don't think, but he was certainly there while we were having the séance. We asked if we could take a photo of him, and he said he was standing by the fireplace at the time. So I took a photo, and when I got the photo developed, there is a strange sort of curly bright light that's coming from the right-hand corner of the photo. I'm not a photography expert, but to me it certainly looks like something was picked up on the film. There's something going on in the house for sure."

Today, Monte Cristo is a well-manicured home, filled with priceless antiques that Reg Ryan has collected over the years and restored to the splendor that it once was. If the setting isn't enough to remind guests what life must have been like for the wealthiest family in town a century ago, Mr. or Mrs. Crawley may just walk up dressed in their finest Victorian-era clothes and let you have a first-hand look. Just hope they don't take you for a servant.

Chapter 14:
MERCY BROWN,
THE RHODE ISLAND VAMPIRE

Mercy Brown's grave is located in Exeter, Rhode Island Historical Cemetery Number 22. The cemetery lies behind the Chestnut Hill Baptist Church on Highway 102. Photo by Jeff Belanger.

MERCY BROWN,
THE RHODE ISLAND VAMPIRE:

Exeter, Rhode Island

Chestnut Hill Cemetery

"There are such beings as vampires; some of us have evidence that they exist. Even had we not the proof of our own unhappy experience, the teachings and the records of the past give proof enough for sane peoples," said Dr. Seward's diary in Bram Stoker's *Dracula*. It was Bram Stoker who took the vampire of folklore and made him beautiful, powerful, and sexy. There were cases of vampires all over the world before, during, and even after *Dracula* both seduced and frightened us—one of these cases was Mercy Brown, the Rhode Island vampire.

Mercy Brown has the distinction of being the last of the North American vampires—at least in the traditional sense. Mercy Lena Brown was a farmer's daughter and an upstanding member of rural Exeter, Rhode Island. She was only 19 years old when she died of consumption on January 17, 1892. On March 17, 1892, Mercy's body was exhumed from the cemetery because members of the community suspected the vampire Mercy Brown was attacking her dying brother, Edwin.

For a deeper understanding of Mercy Brown and vampirism, I spoke with Dr. Michael Bell, a folklorist and author of *Food for the Dead*, a book that explores the folklore and history behind Mercy Brown as well as several other cases of New England vampires. Many people's understanding of what a vampire is comes mostly from Bram

Stoker's work and Anne Rice novels, but the traditional vampire is actually quite different.

So what is a traditional vampire? "Paul Barber wrote a book called *Vampires, Burial, and Death*," Dr. Bell said. "He gives a forensic interpretation of vampire incidents. They're a natural phenomenon that wasn't understood by the people at the time because they didn't really know what happens to the bodies under different conditions. His definition is that a vampire is your classic scapegoat. I think his definition, if I can paraphrase it, is something like: A vampire is a corpse that comes to the attention of a community during a time of crisis, and is taken for the cause of that crisis." Vampires of folklore were not the romantic characters of modern cinema; they were the walking dead who literally drained the life out of their victims. Attacking vampires was a way for a community to physically embody and fight an evil that was plaguing them. In the case of Mercy Brown, that evil was consumption.

During the 1800s, consumption, or pulmonary tuberculosis, was credited with one out of four deaths. Consumption could kill you slowly over many years, or the disease could come quickly and end your life in a matter of weeks. The effects were devastating on families and communities. Dr. Bell explained that some of the symptoms of consumption are the gradual loss of strength and skin tone. The victim becomes pale, stops eating, and literally wastes away. At night, the condition worsens because the patient is lying on their back, and fluid and blood may collect in the lungs. During later stages, one might wake up to find blood on one's face, neck, and nightclothes; breathing is laborious; and the body is starved for oxygen.

Dr. Bell feels there is a direct connection between vampire cases and consumption. He said, "The way you look personally is the way vampires have always been portrayed in folklore—like walking corpses, which is what you are, at least in the later stages of consumption. Skin and bones, fingernails are long and curved, you look like the vampire from *Nosferatu*."

Consumption took its first victim within the Brown family in December of 1883 when Mercy's mother, Mary Brown, died of the disease. Seven months later, the Browns' eldest daughter, Mary Olive, also died of consumption. The Browns' only son, Edwin, came down with consumption a few years after Mary Olive's death and was sent to live in the arid climate of Colorado to try and stop the disease. Late in 1891, Edwin returned home to Exeter because the disease was progressing—he essentially came home to die. Mercy's battle with consumption was considerably shorter than her brother's. Mercy had the "galloping" variety of consumption, and her battle with the disease lasted only a few months. She was laid to rest in Chestnut Hill Cemetery behind the Baptist church on Victory Highway.

After Mercy's funeral, her brother Edwin's condition worsened rapidly, and their father, George Brown, grew more frantic. Mr. Brown had lost his wife and two of his daughters, and now he was about to lose his only son. Science and medicine had no answers for George Brown, but folklore did. For centuries prior to Mercy Brown, there have been vampires. The practice of slaying these "walking dead" began in Europe—some of the ways people dealt with vampires was to exhume the body of the suspect, drive a stake through the heart, rearrange the skeletal remains, remove vital organs, or cremate the entire corpse. All of these rituals involve desecrating the mortal remains. The practice happened with enough regularity that the general population felt it could cure, or at the very least help, whatever evil was overwhelming them.

So much death had plagued the Brown family that poor George Brown probably felt he was cursed in some way. It wouldn't take too many chats with those empathizing with George's plight to come up with a radical idea to stop the death. Maybe the Brown family was under vampire attacks from beyond the grave. Was Mercy Brown the vampire, or was it Mercy's mother or sister? George Brown was willing to dig up the body of his recently deceased daughter, remove her heart, burn it, and feed the ashes to his son because he felt he had no other choice.

In Dr. Bell's book, *Food for the Dead*, he recounts an extensive interview he conducted with Everett Peck, a descendant of Mercy Brown and life-long resident of Exeter, Rhode Island. "Everett heard the story from people who had been there [at the exhumation of Mercy Brown]—who were alive at the time," Dr. Bell said. "The newspaper [*Providence Journal*] says they exhumed all three bodies, that is, Mercy's mother, her sister who had died before her, and Mercy. Everett said they only dug up Mercy. He implied that there was some sign that Mercy was the one—that's the supernatural creeping into his story. Everett said that after they had dug her up, [they saw that] she had turned over in the grave—but there's no mention of that in the newspaper or the eyewitness accounts."

Mercy Brown died before embalming became a common practice. During decomposition, it is possible for bodies to sit up, jerk—even sounds can emit from them because bloating can occur, and if wind escapes, passing over the vocal chords, there could be groans.

We don't know exactly what position her body was in on that day in March when George Brown and some of his friends and family came to examine Mercy's body. We do know that she looked "too well preserved."

"There's a suggestion in the newspaper that she wasn't actually interred in the ground," Dr. Bell said. "She was actually put in an above-ground crypt, because bodies were stored in the wintertime when the ground was frozen and they couldn't really dig. When the thaw came, they would bury them. So it's possible that she wasn't even really interred."

Her visual condition prompted the group to cut open her chest cavity and examine her innards. Dr. Bell said, "They examined her organs. The newspaper said her heart and liver had blood in it. It was liquid blood, which they interpreted as fresh blood." Bell explained how forensics can clarify how blood can coagulate and become liquid again, but at the time, the liquid was taken as evidence that Mercy was indeed a vampire and the one draining the life from Edwin and possibly other consumption victims in the community.

Dr. Bell said, "They cut her heart out, and as Everett said, they burned it on a nearby rock. Then according to the newspaper, they fed them [the ashes of the heart] to Edwin." The folklore said that destroying the heart of a vampire would kill it, and by consuming the remains of the vampire's heart—the spell would be broken and the victim would get well.

The community's vampire slaying had failed to save Edwin—he died two months later—but perhaps it helped others in the community? Dr. Bell's view on Mercy Brown is that she was the scapegoat author Paul Barber discussed. Dr. Bell said, "She basically absorbs the ignorance, the fears, and in some cases the guilt that people have because their neighbors, friends, and family are dying, and they don't understand why and they can't stop it."

Today some claim to see Mercy Brown's specter near her headstone. Others have also spotted a glowing ball of light above her grave. Dr. Bell said, "That's called a 'corpse light' in folklore. That's a well-known phenomenon—it's been reported all over the place. There have been explanations, like the process of decomposing organic matter, like human flesh creating methane gas that can be ignited, and so on, but who knows? Things like that, you feel that there must be something behind it even if you can't explain exactly what it is."

Mercy Brown is arguably North America's most famous vampire because she is also the most recent. The event caused such a stir in 1892 because newspapers such as the *Providence Journal* editorialized that the idea of exhuming a body to burn the heart is completely barbaric in those modern times.

As Dr. Bell said, "Folklore always has an answer—it may not be the scientifically valid answer, but sometimes it's better to have any answer than none at all."

Chapter 15:
Empress Theatre

The Empress Theatre regularly shows the latest Hollywood block-busters, as well as film festivals and live theatres. Contact the theatre for show times and performance schedules. Photo by Stephen Delano.

EMPRESS THEATRE:

Fort Macleod, Alberta

Tel: 1 (800) 540-9229

Web: *www.empresstheatre.ab.ca*

TOP SECRET

In his late 16th-century play, *As You Like It*, William Shakespeare wrote, "All the world's a stage, And all the men and women merely players; They have their exits and their entrances...." As we know from the many ghostly accounts at the Empress Theatre in Fort Macleod, sometimes people do come back after their mortal exit. Many outsiders refer to the source of the Empress Theatre haunting as the "Phantom of the Empress," but to the employees, actors, and volunteers, their Theatre's spirit is simply called "Ed"—their biggest fan.

The Empress Theatre was originally a franchise of the Famous Players theatre chain. J.S. Lambert began construction on his franchise in 1910 on the now historic Main Street during Fort Macleod's boom period. The theater has been home to vaudeville, concerts, lectures, live theater, and moving pictures. A January 1910 *Lethbridge Herald* reported that the new building would be a "first class theatre with every modern accessory." Construction was completed in 1912, and the theater opened to the public.

In 1937, Daniel Boyle bought the Empress and performed some significant renovations. He moved the projection booth above the new 100-seat balcony he installed. He also enclosed the vestibule, added washrooms and the cornerstone of any movie theater, a concession stand. In addition to the new construction, Boyle made decorative enhancements such as updated light fixtures, window covers, and light-up neon tulips on the pressed tin ceiling in honor of his wife.

129

From 1937 to 1982, the building remained unchanged and the theater productions, movies, customers, and time that passed over and through the Empress took their toll on the building. In 1982, the Fort Macleod Provincial Historic Area Society took over the building, and in 1988, the foundation poured more than $1 million into restoring the Empress to the splendor Dan Boyle had established about 50 years prior.

Though there is no record of any deaths at the Empress, the ghostly accounts go back even before 1988, but post-renovations, the activity increased significantly. From 1986 until 1990, Jay Russell worked for the Great West Theatre Company—a group that operated out of the Empress Theatre. He told me about his encounter—one of the first ghost reports from the Empress. "My theory is that once they started renovating, that's when weird things started to happen," Russell said. "The building, of course, is on a cement foundation, but there was kind of a crawl space and gravel bed underneath where the seats were. They started digging out all kinds of really neat old things, like an old movie poster of Tex Ritter, and all this really neat stuff. I think when they started renovating they disturbed something."

Russell's encounter occurred in June of 1988. At the time, he was a university student and trying to work in theater in his summers. Because of a clerical error, he hadn't received a paycheck in months, so he was living as financially lean as possible. When his theater troupe decided on a group lunch, Russell stayed behind and therefore was the only person in the building. "I didn't go, because I was really poor, and I had a lunch. I decided I wasn't going to spend any money; I was going to stay. Besides, it would give me a chance to look around the Theatre. I go down the old wooden stairs—they were really creaky; you could hear someone come down them anytime.

"In the basement, there was a bunch of changing rooms, but they were really tiny. We would use the changing rooms, but there was a bigger area; I think we called it the Boiler Room. It was big enough for us to sit around and wait for our cue. And next to that was what we called the Swamp Cooler Room.

"In the Swamp Cooler Room, there's no light bulb and no switch. The room has a big steel door, and there's no handle on the inside of the door. I propped the door open because I knew there was stuff in there. With the door open, I could see this old organ. It didn't look like it was complete—it looked like it was all broken up. So I started walking toward the organ. I reached into the dark, and it's getting darker and darker, and I have my hand extended out trying to reach this old keyboard or whatever it is. And just as I touch it, there's this big laugh behind me. Like someone is pulling the funniest joke in the world on me. It [the laugh] wasn't spooky; it was just this big belly laugh. And all of a sudden, the prop on my door was gone and the door slams shut. And then *thump, thump, thump, thump* up the stairs. Someone was laughing and running up the stairs. I was so mad. Theater guys are full of pranks and jokes, and after a minute or so they weren't coming back."

I asked Russell if he recognized the voice. He said, "I didn't recognize the laugh. And I would have heard somebody coming down the stairs, and I didn't hear anybody come down, I just heard them go up."

Russell sat in a completely dark and silent room for an hour and a half until the crew returned from lunch. They heard his shouts for help and let him out. Russell said. "They all vouched that they were all together, and no one left lunch."

Diana Segboer was born and raised in Fort Macleod, as were her parents. Segboer was on the management board of the Empress Theatre in various roles, from executive member to General Manager of the theater. "I had always heard about the ghosts even as a kid," Segboer said. "When we would go to the theater as kids, you would hear how there was supposedly things happening, but I didn't experience anything until I started becoming more involved in the operation of the theater."

So what were those early reports? Segboer said, "Several younger kids had seen someone behind them in the mirror. They described him as an older gentleman with very hairy arms."

Diana Segboer's first personal experience at the Empress occurred in the early 1990s, when she went in while the theater was closed to take inventory of the concession booth. She was going to place an order for more supplies. "I walked in through the lobby and went around into the concession booth," she said. "I heard some footsteps coming up the staircase and I thought '*Hmmm*, I thought I was alone, but hey, maybe Mike [another theater employee] was in the building.' The footsteps kept coming and kept coming, and pretty soon I heard them right beside me and then they stopped. And you could feel the air just change—it went from regular air to almost frigid air. I just put down my notepad that I was writing on and I walked out the front door."

The first encounter gave Segboer a good scare, but over time, as more encounters happened to her, she became more used to them and regarded each brush with the supernatural as something very special.

The Empress Theatre has an alarm system complete with motion detectors. In the 1990s, Segboer was the telephone contact for the security monitoring company when the alarm went off. She recalls several trips down to the theater in the middle of the night to meet the police and do a walk-through of the building. One night, Segboer got a phone call from the security company and decided to not ask the police to meet her at the theater because these calls had become routine, and she had a friend with her who could accompany her on her walk-through. Segboer said, "We turned on all of the lights, and we couldn't find anything. Joyce, who was with me, was humming this song. I can't remember the song, but we were walking out the front door and she was humming it. Just as I go to push the door open, he [the ghost] whistled the end of the song. Joyce turned around and she just freaked. She couldn't believe it! She said, 'Did you hear that?' And I said, 'Oh yeah, I heard that.' And we just left. So obviously he was with us when we were doing the inspection."

Stephen Delano is the Summer Theatre Coordinator for the Empress Theatre. He told me about some of the many ghostly goings-on he's heard about at the Empress. "He [the ghost] likes to play with the curtains during performances," Delano said. "Also, we have these large neon tulips on our ceiling, and he likes to play with those—he turns them on and off during performances and things like that."

Due to the innocent, yet prankster nature of some of the ghost happenings, Diana Segboer believes there may also be the spirit of a child or even some children in the Empress. "Sometimes you hear footsteps running down the aisle. It's fast, like [it's being made by] short legs," she said. The seats of the theater have also been toyed with. The Empress Theatre has pretty standard theater seats that fold up to allow more aisle access between rows, but these seats are not spring-loaded. When the seats are up they stay up, and when they're down, they stay down...usually. "I was upstairs in the balcony and was putting the seats up, and in the next row, the row that I had just finished, they were coming down as fast as I was putting them up. One by one," Segboer said.

The balcony is where actors in the theater's live productions have reported seeing an old, burly gentleman with hairy arms sitting in the same seat during performances. After a short while, the man disappears. When the actors ask around later, no one in the audience can say they saw anyone in the vicinity of where the actors saw this man. He was only visible to a select few on stage.

The theater's ghost pulls other pranks as well. Delano said, "He likes to take garbage right out of the garbage can. People have said they'll go and pick up a piece of garbage and throw it away, then come back a few minutes later and it will be in the same spot as before."

One popular theory as to the identity of the Phantom of the Empress is that it's Dan Boyle, because the activity didn't start until the renovations began, and the common supernatural occurrences tend to be more managerial in style, such as toying with the curtains, the neon lights, the seats, and so on. But there is a second suspect. Delano said, "It could be a janitor who worked here in the 1950s. This janitor had a second job at the auction market in Fort Macleod. He was mysteriously found dead one night at the auction market, and no one knows how he died. A lot of people think it's this guy, because he was a bit of an alcoholic, he worked at the auction market, and he was a cigar smoker. It seems to be that often when there's a ghost experience, it's followed by the smell of alcohol, manure, or cigar smoke. That's why a lot of people think it's this guy."

Diana Segboer agrees that the ghost is most likely the janitor. She explained why, "I can remember Dan Boyle. I remember him when I was little and I used to go to the theater, and he was a very small man. It's pretty much the exact opposite of what has been described." When Segboer described the large, hairy-armed man to her parents when she first heard about the ghost as a child, her father believed the description fit the janitor who was mysteriously murdered in the 1950s near the auction market.

Another common occurrence is that patrons come in and buy their tickets from an elderly gentleman at the ticket booth, and then they find out later that only a woman was working at the ticket booth that night. For decades now, someone has been watching over the performances, the building, and the people inside. No one feels threatened by this presence, and he's become one of the actors' favorite fans. To "Ed," all the Empress Theatre is his stage.

Chapter 16:
THORNEWOOD CASTLE

Thornewood Castle is a private residence that operates as a bed-and-breakfast. Additionally, the owners occasionally run history and ghost tours through the property. Check with the Castle for details. Photo courtesy of Thornewood Castle.

THORNEWOOD CASTLE:

Lakewood, Washington

Tel: 1 (253) 584-4393

Web: *www.thornewoodcastle.com*

Thornewood Castle is a 16th-century medieval English castle located at the edge of American Lake on the outskirts of Tacoma, Washington in the U.S. Pacific Northwest. How, you ask? In 1908, Tacoma business mogul Chester Thorne invested $1 million to build his dream house. He wanted to capture the essence of an English manor home in Washington. To make his dream come true, architect Kirtland Kelsey Cutter would get most of the brick, stone, oak paneling, oak staircases, and stained glass by dismantling a castle in England and shipping the materials via three cargo ships around the treacherous waters of Cape Horn in South America, all the way up the coast of the Americas to the port of Tacoma. After three years of building, the dream home was completed.

Born in 1863 in Thornedale, New York, Chester A. Thorne came from a wealthy family of financiers—he was a Yale graduate who got his start in business with the Missouri Pacific Railway Company. Thorne married the company general manager's daughter, Anna, and moved to Tacoma, Washington, where he invested money in the National Bank of Commerce. By age 30, he became the bank's president. Thorne, a meticulous businessman, acquired significant wealth and prestige as one of the founders of the Port of Tacoma, and he was one of the driving forces behind the founding of Mount Rainier National Park. The Thornewood Castle was a giant monument to his prosperity.

The 27,000-square-foot English Tudor/Gothic mansion has 54 rooms, including 28 bedrooms and 22 baths. The Thornes had 68 people working at the estate—28 gardeners, as well as 40 house servants to care for Chester, Anna, and their daughter, Anita.

Thornewood was the place for American dignitaries to visit. Besides many prominent businessmen in the Pacific Northwest, overnight guests included Presidents Theodore Roosevelt and William Howard Taft and even some foreign royalty. Ches, as those who knew him best called him, had not only made a lot of money, he also made a lot of friends in the community through his works of charity. He had a great life for sure and Thornewood Castle was his masterpiece. Ches died of a lingering illness on October 16, 1927 in his palatial mansion, but Thornewood would always be Ches's house.

I spoke with Deanna Robinson, the current owner of Thornewood. Deanna and her husband, Wayne, bought the estate in April 2000, and very soon after, they made an agreement with ABC Disney to allow the company to film Stephen King's *Rose Red* miniseries there. In exchange for allowing the property to be used as the setting for King's story of a paranormal researcher who takes a team of psychics into a haunted house, ABC Disney agreed to remove the apartments that were installed in the Great Hall and the Ballroom and restore them to their original splendor.

In King's story, the house has its own consciousness and the building is constantly shifting and changing—but the truth, as they say, is usually stranger than fiction. The house doesn't mystically grow new staircases that climb to nowhere, and rooms don't shrink, but there is a hidden room, tunnels in the basement, and a spirit to the house itself. In addition, there are multiple ghosts who manifest themselves all over.

Robinson and her many guests rave about the unexplainable yet revitalizing energy with which Thornewood Castle affects people.

The ghostly activity started very subtly for Robinson. She said, "We were using the Gentleman's Parlor for a breakfast room for just my husband and I—it was just right off the kitchen. I would turn all the lights down in the evening, and when I would come down in the mornings to turn on the wall sconce lighting, on one of the wall sconces the light bulb was out. So I went to change the light bulb. I got my little stool, because it's too tall for me to reach. When I reached for the bulb, I realized it was just unscrewed. So I screwed it back in and went away. At night I turned off the light, locked the room, and went to bed. The next morning I got up and came downstairs, and the light bulb is unscrewed again. I thought that was really strange. I got my little ladder again, climbed up, and screwed it back in.

"This went on every day for two weeks. So finally, I had a little pad of paper in my hand, and I threw it on the table and said, 'Okay, Chester. I know you're here. Leave me a note, because I'm sick and tired of this light bulb bit!'"

No note was left, but the daily unscrewing of the bulb did stop, though not for long. Apparently, one of the spirits of Thornewood has a fixation with glass. Robinson assumes it's Chester but can't be certain, but the glass problem did escalated from just the light bulbs. Robinson explained how her husband bought a set of stainless steel pots and pans with metal-rimmed glass lids. She said, "We had them put away in a cabinet. We were in the kitchen not really doing anything, and there was this huge explosion in the cabinet. We kind of eased up to the cabinet and opened it, and a glass frying pan lid had just broken into thousands of pieces. It exploded."

The event repeated itself on another date with an expensive glass punch bowl. "We hadn't put anything in it; we just set it on the counter," Robinson said. "It was sitting there and the whole thing just breaks. And when it broke, it just fell into little piles of glass."

On another occasion, her grandson was carrying some bottles of liquor up from storage, and he had one bottle tucked under his arm. The bottom of the glass bottle popped out, and the booze spilled all over Robinson's grandson and the floors.

Robinson believes a lot of the disturbances may occur because she has had so much construction and restoration done, and Chester Thorne may not have liked some woman messing with his house. She's careful not to accuse him of being a chauvinist, but she says she believes Chester eventually liked the results and he doesn't break the glass anymore. She said, "We're not having as much these days. We hear breakage, but there's nothing broken when we look around."

Robinson may have received some conformation that Chester was pleased with her efforts from her groundskeeper—an ex-military man who had worked at the property since before the Robinsons took ownership. Robinson said, "He came in one day and told me that Mr. Thorne approved of what I was doing with the house. And he claims to have seen him a number of times on the lawn in a brown riding suit with jockey spurs."

The man in the brown riding suit with fancy pockets and spurs, carrying a short, leather riding crop, has also been spotted in the house. The Robinsons had a friend from Texas up to stay with them, and Deanna asked her friend to go to a closet in the third floor to get some soap. Her friend was rifling through the closet trying to find the soap when she turned around to see the man in the brown riding suit. He asked her, "What are you doing here?" And she said, half-frantic, "I don't know what I'm doing here. I just came to get something for Deanna…" The man vanished and Robinson's friend came running downstairs, pale-faced and with an experience she'll never forget.

Photo courtesy of Thornewood Castle.

Thornewood is also a setting for weddings and receptions. One of their suites, called "Anna's Room," after the late madam of the house who used the room as her bedroom, is also the bridal suite. There is a full-length mirror in the room and plenty of space for a bride to get ready. Several brides have reported seeing the reflection of a woman dressed in early 20th-century clothing in the mirror sitting in a seat behind them. When the brides turn around, they find the woman gone.

Other guests have also seen a woman in the room. Robinson said, "We've had people in the garden see a woman standing in that room by the window. And it's the room they're staying in. And our guests have the only keys to the room—there's no housekeeper, so it couldn't have been anyone else."

In 2001, the Robinsons brought in the Washington State Ghost Society (WSGS) to conduct an investigation of the hauntings. The WSGS is a collection of people who investigate the paranormal on a part-time basis. The group is comprised of researchers, some psychically sensitive people, and others who want to learn more. Henry Bailey was the group's founder and president. Bailey's day job was working for Boeing at the time, and he explained how he tries to avoid the subjective when he can—his main interests lie with measurable facts. He said, "I'm an engineer by profession. I never claimed to be psychic, but the area around Thornewood does have one of the most peaceful and calm auras, I guess you'd call it, that I've ever felt in my life. It's so revitalizing—it's so subjective to say that, but it actually feels that way."

Bailey explained how his group didn't witness any visible manifestations during their four visits to Thornewood, but they did capture some compelling audio on tape. Bailey sat in the mansion's kitchen at 3:30 a.m., with his audio recorder, trying to obtain an electronic voice phenomenon (EVP). "The best evidence we had were the recordings that we got," Bailey said. "There was one of a man singing in the kitchen. I can vouch that nobody was in the kitchen at that time. I didn't hear anything until I got home and played that tape. The song was a *la-la-la-la*. This was really distinct and clear on the tape."

Bailey believes there is some residual energy leftover from the medieval building materials that could be causing some of the ghost sightings. In addition, he feels there are probably two spirits that do occasionally, and deliberately, interact with the staff and guests of Thornewood. After growing up in three separate haunted houses as a kid, Bailey's conclusion on Thornewood is that all the signs are there for a haunting. Plus, "The house just feels haunted—I'll put it that way," he said.

There is an oak staircase near the main entrance of the house, which is a particularly active spot to catch a ghostly glimpse of the past. "If you sit on the bottom stair of the staircase and look at the doors, sometimes you'll catch a glimpse of a Lord and Lady," Robinson said of the couples that sometimes appear. "The men are wearing leather and kind of smell oily—I think they think they're dressed up, but it's not what we would consider real clean today. I've seen two women—one with a garland in her hair and the other with kind of a pointed cap on—wearing Renaissance clothing, and they come through the doors and then go away."

For the Thorne family, the castle's creation was a masterful blend of old and new. It's a place where 16th-century England collided with 20th-century America. Today, Thornewood is also a place where the physical and spiritual planes occasionally blend. For Deanna Robinson and her guests, the palatial home, manicured lawns, and lush gardens are paradise. One can understand why the original builder and his family may never want to leave.

Chapter 17:
THE SKIRRID MOUNTAIN INN

Located in Llanvihangel Crucorney, a parish near the town of Abergavenny, in Monmouthshire County, The Skirrid Mountain Inn public house is open Monday through Saturday, 11 a.m. to 11 p.m., and Sunday, noon to 10:30 p.m. They also have three rooms available for nightly rentals. Photo courtesy of the Skirrid Mountain Inn.

THE SKIRRID MOUNTAIN INN:

Llanvihangel Crucorney, Wales

Tel: 44 (0) 1873-890258

Web: *myweb.tiscali.co.uk/skirrid/*

The Skirrid Mountain Inn lies at the base of Skirrid Mountain—a 1600-foot-tall peak that legend says was split in half by a terribly violent storm at the very moment of the Crucifixion of Christ. The mountain has seen millennia of Welsh history: wars, the birth of empires, the struggle of religious powers, and the rise of villages to cities. Like the mountain that is the Inn's namesake, the public house at the mount's base has also seen violent storms throughout its more than nine centuries of history. In its stairwell, 182 people were executed by hanging. With such a long and occasionally dark history, the pub is not only one of the oldest, but also one of the most haunted places in the United Kingdom.

The first written record of the building's existence dates back to 1104 C.E., though its owners believe the building is even older, and they hope some currently ongoing research soon proves that. The Skirrid has always been a public house, and because of its remote location, many times the premises doubled as a courtroom and even gallows for local criminals during the period between the 12th and 17th centuries. Inside the Skirrid Inn, visitors are greeted by brick fireplaces and large oak beams supporting the second story. The beams, made from ship's timbers, still show the slots and peg holes where they were fitted to each other.

The Inn's central staircase most prominently displays the beam construction. The staircase features a series of rises, landings, and turns, so one can see why the beams are a very convenient place to hang a rope. Halfway up the stairs sits a small room that was used to hold the prisoners overnight before their hanging in the morning. One can only imagine the torment of sitting in a small room, listening to the sounds of a lively pub below you, knowing that, in the morning, you'd be taking a short walk down a few steps to your death.

Near the bottom of the staircase, visitors can still see where the hangman's rope wore away a notch in the wooden beam. The feet of the unlucky victims wouldn't have been more than a foot or so from the bottom step—meaning there were no quick deaths by the snap of the neck. Those found guilty slowly choked and suffocated to death. In 1110, the first man sentenced to hang in the pub was John Crowther, accused of stealing sheep.

The vast majority of hangings at the Skirrid were also some of the earliest instances of ethnic cleansing in the world. In 1685, the Duke of Monmouth led the Monmouth rebellion. He was a Protestant and the bastard son of Charles II, and some of his countrymen urged him to take the throne from the Catholic King James II. The uprising failed, and in the aftermath, King James II sent his judges to try and condemn all who were involved in the attempted treason. One of these judges, "Hanging" Judge Jeffreys, was the most feared in all of Britain. He sentenced more than 200 people throughout Britain to death for crimes as minor as even knowing one of the rebels. This further fueled an anti-Catholic backlash in Abergavenny. Ultra-Protestant Squire John Arnold of Llanvihangel Court was anti-Catholic to his core, and he allegedly sent many Papists to their death on the rope in the Skirrid Mountain Inn. Local legends say Judge Jeffries came to the Skirrid to put a stop to the backlash. Daryl Hardy, the Inn's current co-owner said, "They think he stayed over at Llanvihangel Court, because there was a tunnel that came from the Court to the pub. And he used to come to work that way so that he wouldn't get bumped off coming across land." *Llanvihangel* is a Welsh word meaning "near the church of St. Michael."

The final hanging at the Skirrid took place near the end of the 17th century. Ironically, the crime perpetrated was stealing sheep—the same offense as for its first hanging.

In the late 18th to early 19th century, the Price family owned and operated the Skirrid. The Price family is worth noting, because it's this family to which many attribute the ghosts. Landlady Fanny Price died of consumption in the Inn's smallest bedroom, in the early 1800s. She and other members of the Price family have their eternal resting places in the churchyard just a short distance from the pub. "She walks the pub at night," Hardy said. "Apparently, one of the other major characters in the pub—we can't tell whether it was her father or her husband—but he's called Henry Price. He pretends to be soldiers marching up and down outside on the cobbles—you can hear sort of horses' hooves outside on the cobbles. Or he'll be up in the loft banging on the chimney breasts, trying to scare the guests."

The popular UK television show *Most Haunted* paid a visit to the Skirrid Mountain Inn, and the show's psychic, Derek Acorah, channeled a resident spirit just outside the front door of the Inn. "He actually was taken over by Henry Price," Hardy said, who personally witnessed the event during the filming. "He was running up and down the road outside, screaming and shouting."

Daryl Hardy and his business partner, Maria Appleton, knew nothing of the Inn's haunted nature when they purchased the business in late 2002. There were news clips that ran in October of 2002 by the BBC, where former landlady Heather Grant commented on her ghostly wards. In the article she said: "There have been lots of spooky goings-on since I've been here. I live on my own, and when I first moved in, I have to confess that I was pretty unnerved by things happening. Despite everything that happens here, you do get used to it, and I don't mind them anymore."

Hardy and Appleton didn't see the articles on the Skirrid; they simply saw the property, made an offer, and, four weeks later, moved into the pub near Abergavenny—a town of maybe 60 houses in all.

Soon after moving in, Hardy noticed he simply couldn't keep the pint glasses for the beer intact at the bar. He said, "Glasses are a nightmare for us. We can't fill our shelves from the back to the front, because the front line of glasses just gets wiped off—they fall, are pushed, whatever. We can lose 10 to 15 glasses a week. It's a good thing we don't have to pay for them—the brewers supply them."

Breaking of glasses is not the only peculiar happening at the Inn's bar. Hardy said there were several witnesses to some money moving by an unseen force on the bar. He said, "I saw a £10 note travel the full length of the bar. The habit over here is that customers put their £20 notes down to buy the first round. You put a £10 note down and the change on the top, and you just pick at the money as they order more drinks. This £10 note had change on it. I think it had about £3.50 in change on top of the £10 note. It traveled the full length of the bar and then kept going and went out about 2 feet past the bar before it dropped to the floor. And that was witnessed by about eight to 10 people."

One of the funnier encounters took place in one of the Inn's three guest rooms. An overnight guest complained that he couldn't sleep because the toilet paper roll was spinning itself all night. It didn't unfurl; it just kept spinning and tormenting the poor gentleman who was trying to sleep.

On another occasion, Hardy had gone away for a few days, so his manager stayed overnight in one of the guest rooms with her boyfriend. Hardy said, "Her boyfriend has false teeth. He took his false teeth out and went to bed at night. He woke up in the morning, and they were on the other side of the room in two halves—snapped. He's not overly keen on staying again."

The Skirrid Mountain Inn isn't the only ghost story in Abergavenny. There is a 17th-century manor house, called Llanvihangel Court, in town that is tied to the Skirrid. Similar construction methods were used on both buildings; for example, the two buildings' front doors are identical.

Local lore says that, around the year 1700, the Lord of the manor house was having a fling with a servant girl from the Skirrid. The Lord's wife came home one evening to discover her husband and his mistress, and she chased the girl out of the house and into the woods, eventually giving up when she lost sight of the young home-wrecking lass. The next day, the locals found the girl frozen and sitting against a tree. She'd never made it back to the pub. Today the woods around Abergavenny are called the "White Lady Woods" because of the frequent sightings of a white lady floating through the woods, who locals believe to be the specter of the servant girl still making her final dash from the manor house to the Skirrid Inn. "A lot of people see apparitions, especially on sort of misty winter nights," Hardy said.

The atmosphere of the Skirrid Mountain Inn is reminiscent of another time, though sometimes that older time still makes a guest appearance. The Inn has been a great pub to hang around in for centuries, but if you stop in for a pint, keep a watchful eye on your money on the bar.

Chapter 18:
ARCHER AVENUE'S
RESURRECTION MARY

Resurrection Cemetery is located in the suburb of Justice, southwest of Chicago. Photo by Lisa M. Roppolo.

ARCHER AVENUE'S RESURRECTION MARY:

Justice, Illinois

Resurrection Cemetery

"On a wild Chicago night, with a wind howling white / I caught my first sign of Resurrection Mary" are some words from Ian Hunter's song, "Resurrection Mary," from his 1996 album, *The Artful Dodger*. The story of Chicago's most famous ghost is so widely known that it even influenced a British classic-rocker.

Hunter's song is a case of art imitating real life. It is on cold Chicago nights that the specter of a 1920s-era, blond, bobbed-haired, blue-eyed beauty wearing a white cocktail dress is seen along Archer Avenue, and on some occasions she's been given a ride by cab drivers, police, and motorists who all watch her disappear when she gets near the cemetery.

The 1920s were roaring in Chicago. Prohibition was in full force, speakeasies were run by notorious mobsters such as Al Capone and John Torrio, and dance halls were swinging to the sounds of jazz. It was a time of decadence, parties, dressing to the nines, and painting the town with your dame.

In Willow Springs (another suburb of Chicago), at 8900 Archer Avenue, stood the Oh Henry Ballroom. Built in 1921 by the Verderbar family, it was known as the "country club of ballrooms." Downtown Chicago buses and streetcars had stops in front of Oh Henry's doors. It was at the Oh Henry that the story of Resurrection Mary begins, sometime in the late 1920s.

Mary was out for an evening of dancing with her boyfriend at the Oh Henry Ballroom. After an argument with her beau, she stormed out of the dance hall and started hitchhiking down Archer Avenue, trying to get herself home. She was apparently killed after being struck by a passing motorist and was allegedly buried at Resurrection Cemetery—in her favorite white dress and dancing shoes.

Resurrection Cemetery is a relatively modern Catholic cemetery. Its earliest headstones date back to the 1890s. There's a grand entrance on Archer Avenue with wrought iron gates hinged on cement pillars. The center of the cemetery is dominated by a large mausoleum, and the grounds have numerous shrines. The setting is almost park-like.

I spoke with author Troy Taylor, who has written about Resurrection Mary in several of his books. He claims the earliest sightings happened around 1928 or 1929. She is most often spotted in the winter months of December, January, and February, which leads Taylor to believe she may have died during that time period.

Though there were occasional sightings of a pale woman hitchhiking along Archer Avenue in the late 1920s and early 1930s, the most profound Mary encounter would happen to Jerry Palus in 1939. According to Troy Taylor, Palus had been out of town for a while and hadn't really heard of the legends of Resurrection Mary yet. One night in the winter, Palus went out dancing at the Liberty Grove and Hall, which was located near 47th and South Mozart Street. He never recalled seeing the striking blond walk in, but when he turned around, she was there. He would recall in later interviews how her skin felt cold, and at the end of the evening, when he kissed her, her lips were also clammy. As the evening ended, the woman asked Palus for a ride home and gave him an address. Once the two got into Palus's car, she said she wanted to go down Archer Avenue, a route that was significantly out of the way from the address she gave.

When the two drove past the gates of Resurrection Cemetery, Mary asked Palus to stop the car. He reported that he was confused as to why this woman wanted to get out of the car at this spot. Palus reported the woman saying, "This is where I have to get out, but where I'm going, you can't follow."

Palus was puzzled as he watched the woman run toward the cemetery gates and literally vanish before his eyes.

The next day, Palus drove to the address he was given by the woman the night before. The woman at the house informed him that he could not have been with the striking beauty the night before because she had been dead for more than 10 years. Palus then saw a portrait of the woman he danced with in the home. Years later, Palus was no longer able to recall the address he drove to the next day, but the rest of the details of the evening stayed with him.

Taylor commented on how Palus never made any money on his tale, and never tried to exploit what happened. Jerry Palus died in 1992, never changing his story.

Resurrection Mary is such a part of Chicago folklore that it can be difficult to know who to believe and who is just looking for attention. Taylor spoke of another Resurrection Mary encounter that was told to him. He said, "I did have a guy who contacted me a year or so ago, and he told me that he and his girlfriend were driving along Archer Avenue one night, and they had seen a woman on the side of the road in a white dress that kind of lurched out at them toward their car and then vanished. What was interesting about the story was that his girlfriend was the one who really reacted the most. She was a recent immigrant from some Slovakian country, she had recently come to this country, and she barely even spoke English. She had never heard anything about Resurrection Mary before, and yet she had seen her. I found that to be a little more convincing compared to some of the other stories told."

In the January 31, 1979 *Chicago Tribune*, an article by reporter Bill Geist quoted a local cab driver who would only go by the name of Ralph. Ralph explains how he got lost after dropping off a fare just after midnight on a Thursday in mid-January 1979, and he turned onto Archer Avenue to try and figure out where he was. According to Geist's report, Ralph said, "And there she was. She was standing there with no coat on by the entrance to this little shopping center. No coat! And it was one of those real cold ones, too. She didn't put out her thumb or nothing like that. She just looked at my cab. Of course, I stopped. I figured maybe she had car trouble or something.

"She hopped right in the front seat. She had on this fancy kind of white dress, like she'd just been to a wedding or something, and those new kind of disco-type shoes, with the straps and that. She was a looker. A blond. I didn't have ideas or like that; she was young enough to be my daughter—21, tops..."

Ralph went on to explain how the girl seemed to be very distant, she said nothing except, "The snow came early this year."

Ralph continued: "A couple miles up Archer there [by the cemetery], she jumped with a start, like a horse, and said, 'Here! Here!' I hit the brakes. I looked around and didn't see no kind of house. 'Where?' I said. And then she sticks out her arm and points across the road to my left and says, 'There!' And that's when it happened.

"I looked to my left, like this, at this little shack. And when I turned she was gone. Vanished! And the car door never opened. May the good Lord strike me dead, it never opened."

It's difficult to pinpoint Resurrection Mary for any kind of investigation because she's been spotted all along the 2 1/2-mile stretch of Archer Avenue between Resurrection Cemetery and the Oh Henry Ballroom (now the Willowbrook Ballroom). Dale Kaczmarek is president of the Ghost Research Society, author of *Windy City Ghosts* (Whitechapel Productions, 2000) , and has been researching the supernatural since 1975. I spoke to Kaczmarek about his findings on Resurrection Mary. He has noticed a decrease in Mary sightings since the mid-1990s. He attributes the lower frequency of manifestations to, as one possibility, the street lights being installed by the city, making Archer Avenue a much brighter place at night. But there is another possibility. He said, "We've known for decades that ghosts kind of go through a dormant state for periods of time for no apparent reason. And then suddenly a new rash of sightings may show up. It could be they're kind of recharging their own internal batteries, so to speak. Because to generate a physical apparition or something you can see with the naked eye, we assume, takes a tremendous amount of energy. Much more so than simply creating a cold spot, a sound, or a fragrance. There have also been reports of people actually touching her, saying she's ice cold to the touch. That takes a lot of energy."

Resurrection Mary has also left physical evidence of her presence. In the early 1980s, a man drove by and thought he saw a woman who was locked in the cemetery after it closed. The witness didn't think it was a ghost; he thought someone was stuck in the cemetery and needed help getting out, so he went to the police station to ask some officers for help. The officers went back and didn't see anyone, but they did find the iron bars next to the cemetery gate had been bent by what looked like human hands. The bars were blackened and burned, and there were indents that looked like fingers.

Kaczmarek said, "The Cemetery had their own story. They said this was caused by a front-end loader truck doing some sewer work that had backed into the bars, and they later attempted to straighten the bars using a blowtorch [to heat the bars until they were malleable] and asbestos gloves [to bend them back into proper position]. If you look at how high the marks are off the ground, it's impossible for a truck to back in and only bend that small section. If a truck backed in, it probably would've scratched most of the bars, made some sort of indentations or marks on the bars. It wouldn't pull certain bars in and push other bars in the opposite direction. The marks that were first on there were not blowtorch marks. Later there were blowtorch marks, and an asbestos glove does not leave behind fingerprints. It's just as simple as that."

"They have a strict no-ghost policy at Resurrection Cemetery," said Taylor. "Let me tell you, they want nothing to do with it at all." Resurrection Cemetery is a Catholic cemetery run by the Chicago Arch Diocese. Taylor said that when Joseph Cardinal Bernadin was alive and in charge of the diocese, he was allowing paranormal investigators into Resurrection Cemetery to explore where Mary may be. Since Bernadin's death in November of 1996, the gates have been closed to ghost hunters at night.

From the mid-1970s to present day, Resurrection Mary sightings were getting a bit more frightening. Several people who drive along Archer Avenue have reported a woman in white darting in front of their cars. Some have said their car struck the girl but they could not find a body, while others said the specter passed right through the vehicle. Taylor said, "Right across from the Cemetery, there's a place called Chet's Melody Lounge. I had a chance to talk to Chet Prusinski when he was alive. He used to say that people would come in all the time and tell him 'I was out driving, and as I was driving along, there was this girl who came running out in front of us. We tried to stop and couldn't—we hit her.'"

Taylor recounted a story Prusinski had told him about a trucker who ran into the bar, frantic. Taylor said, "One night Chet was leaving the bar about 3 a.m., and a truck driver pulled in. The guy was really in hysterics, telling Chet he hit this girl on the road and now he couldn't find her, and what was he going to do? It was all Chet could do to convince this guy you really didn't hit anybody. The driver was so sure that this actually happened."

Resurrection Mary is a classic American ghost story, but who exactly was Mary? Paranormal researchers have combed through the cemetery and did find a headstone with the name "Mary Bregovy" on it who died on March 10, 1934. Though the first name is a match, and the time period is close to when sightings were starting to be reported, Mary Bregovy was a black-haired woman who died in downtown Chicago, not along Archer Avenue.

The question of who Resurrection Mary really was will probably never be answered, but she is a fixture on Chicago's South side to this day. Anyone driving by the cemetery on Archer Avenue on a cold, winter night can't help but look for a blond woman in a white cocktail dress. She may be shivering in the cold, or she may be waiting to cut one last rug at one of the local dance halls. Enjoy her company before she disappears.

Chapter 19:
BILLY BISHOP LEGION HALL

The Billy Bishop Legion Hall is open seven days a week, 11:30 a.m. to midnight, to its members and guests. Tours are offered, but it's a good idea to call ahead to make sure someone is available to show you around. Photo by Christopher Pallin.

BILLY BISHOP LEGION HALL:

Vancouver, British Columbia

Tel: 1 (604) 738-4142

Web: *www.royalcanadianlegion.com*

Some ghosts haunt where they died, others haunt where they lived, but once in a while, it seems we come across a ghost who haunts where she's needed. No deaths have ever been reported at the Billy Bishop, yet supernatural accounts still abound.

The Billy Bishop Legion Hall is the Vancouver branch of the Royal Canadian Legion. Inside are literally hundreds of pieces of memorabilia, mainly from the Canadian armed services, but there are also some plaques, medals, and other tidbits of military history from foreign countries. For many years now, there have been reports of strange banging, knocking, and even a ghost sighting inside the legion hall. In one corner of the first floor, where the lights flicker and some claim to sense a presence, there's a piece of artwork that some have dubbed "the haunted painting." The hall's upper floor has produced even more ghostly activity.

The building that would go on to become the Billy Bishop Legion Hall was originally a clubhouse for an athletic group called the Meralomas. Construction began in the spring of 1929 and was completed for a July 25, 1930 opening. In 1936, the Canadian Pacific Railway bought the land and its building, but because of the Great Depression, payments were missed and the city of Vancouver took over the building. In 1947, the Air Force Association (AFA) bought the Meralomas' clubhouse, and the building got its start as a veteran's club.

Through some consolidations of veterans' organizations, the AFA would be rolled into an organization called the Canadian Legion, in 1958, and ultimately into the Royal Canadian Legion, in 1960. Because the group's membership was dwindling, it was decided that enrollment would be opened to all branches of the Canadian armed services.

In 1964, the legion hall was named the "Billy Bishop" in honor of the top Allied flying ace during World War I, William Avery "Billy" Bishop. Bishop hailed from Owen Sound, Ontario, and was understandably a Canadian national hero after downing 70 enemy aircraft.

John Macdonald has been a member of the Billy Bishop since 1982 and is currently the public relations contact for the hall. He told me he started hearing about some of the ghostly happenings around 1995, but since he started taking note of the accounts and asking around, he's also found reports that date back to the 1970s. "There is a corner that people get a rather weird feeling in, when they're sitting there," Macdonald said. "Nobody has really seen anything, but there is a painting that's not finished, because the fellow who painted it went back east to visit relatives and he died. So he was never able to finish the painting."

The painting, in the northeast corner of the building, is of three dress-uniformed members of the King's Troop, Royal Horse Artillery on horseback, towing a cannon. The trees in the background are unfinished. We've heard of ghosts sticking around because of unfinished business, and in the case of the haunted painting, we're being quite literal. Maybe the painter's spirit feels some anguish about the brushstrokes still needed to complete the artwork. "I think that has something to do with the way people feel about this little corner," Macdonald said. "My friend Mark was in one afternoon on a Saturday, and our bartender was at the bar. They were the only two people here. The bartender was doing a crossword puzzle, and Mark was doing some paperwork. He went to the bathroom, came back out, and the light in the corner was off. It's one of two lights in the lower building that is on its own switch, and he had to go and switch it back on." Neither Mark nor the bartender witnessed anyone shutting the lights off.

The regulars of the Billy Bishop agree that most of the supernatural activity takes place upstairs. In the 1970s, a former Legion president named Ted was the first to open up one morning, and he heard people walking upstairs. He climbed the steps to investigate, but found nothing. On the first Saturday in April 2002, one of the Billy Bishop employees came in to open up the bar. After walking through the front door and turning off the motion-detecting alarm, she started getting the hall ready for the day. Macdonald said, "She came in, made coffee, and heard hammering upstairs. She thought our archivist must be repairing paintings or plaques. She went upstairs to tell him that she made fresh coffee. But there was no one there. That was 11:30 in the morning. By the time I got here at 2:00 in the afternoon, she was still shaking like a leaf. She could hardly pour the beer."

There are about 650 members of the Billy Bishop today, and like many legion halls, they do rent out their space for different causes. The Billy Bishop has been letting out a room for weekly Alcoholics Anonymous (AA) meetings since the 1950s. I spoke with a long-time Vancouver resident we're going to call "George," who was an active member of the AA meetings at the Billy Bishop. His supernatural experience illustrated that not all ghost encounters are scary; in fact, sometimes they can be really touching.

George first started going to AA in the 1950s, but after a few years, he stopped going to meetings. In the 1970s, he decided to go back and give the program another chance. He walked into the upper floor of the Billy Bishop for an evening meeting. George said, "I hadn't been there in about 20 years. A lot of the founding members were still alive at that time. There was a seat vacant next to me, and this woman by the name of Beulah, she came and sat there beside me as the meeting got started." George explained how Beulah was one of the founders of AA in Vancouver; she was also one of the people who played a significant role in helping and encouraging him when he first got into the program some 20 years prior. For the first 30 to 40 minutes of the meeting, Beulah didn't say anything, but she smiled and nodded at what people were saying.

George continued: "Coffee time came, kind of like a halftime, and I was going to go have a coffee with her, but she wasn't there. I asked people around me, 'Has Beulah been around for a while?' They said, 'She's been dead for about 10 years.' I couldn't believe it. She was sitting right next to me. She was a really saintly person. She worked with AA members all of her life. She sponsored a lot of people. She was one of my favorites. I just couldn't believe it."

George still isn't sure if he believes in ghosts, but he certainly can't explain what he saw. Maybe Beulah was there to be a familiar face to help George back into AA. It's remarkable that this kind woman who had helped so many others with their addiction was there for more than a half an hour, next to George, before she mysteriously vanished. Today, AA meetings are still held at the Billy Bishop.

According to John Macdonald, others have also sensed the presence of a spirit on the upper floor of the legion hall. He said, "There is a spot upstairs where there are three windows on the north side. I can take up people that have psychic abilities, or at least claim to, and about 50 to 60 percent of them will point to a spot between two windows. Most people say it's a short woman that they can feel."

The land that the building rests on was very close to a Squamish Indian village before the rail came and Vancouver was completely industrialized and colonized. There's no logical reason why the Billy Bishop should be haunted, but ghosts are used to defying logic.

Still, the strange sounds from the upstairs continue, and no one can explain why. Macdonald said, "People hear things moving, furniture being dragged, footsteps. One night two friends of mine were here and I had just left. The bartender had come up to make sure the place was all closed up—all the windows were properly latched, and doors latched. They went down and then heard people walking around upstairs. They went up to see what was going on, and there was nothing."

Strange goings-on happen once every two to three weeks, according to Macdonald. The activity can be as subtle as lights flickering or as distinct as the sound of an unseen hammer banging. The events have taken place both day and night.

Though the ghost of the artist may not be able to pick up a brush to put the finishing touches on his incomplete painting, he seems to find creative ways to get attention from the afterlife, by toying with lights or making strange sounds in the building. The spirit of the kind woman upstairs seems intent on sitting back and watching the people come and go through the Billy Bishop, waiting for a chance to help someone through a tough time.

Chapter 20:
SOUTH BRIDGE
UNDERGROUND VAULTS

Though the underground vaults of Edinburgh are vast, the section that visitors can tour is partially owned by Mercat Tours. Tours through the vaults are offered daily. Private tours can also be arranged. Photo courtesy of Mercat Tours.

SOUTH BRIDGE UNDERGROUND VAULTS:

Edinburgh, Scotland

Tel: 44 (0) 131-557-6464

Web: *www.mercattours.com/tours/*
haunted_underground.htm

The underground vaults of Edinburgh, Scotland, are vast, man-made caverns where the working class once labored and lived. Over time, the shortsighted workmanship of the South Bridge that spans the city's Cowgate ravine allowed the Edinburgh rains to seep below, into the living areas, spreading diseases such as consumption and cholera. The city council deemed the area unfit for habitation, and then the darker side of humanity moved in. After decades of brothels, dens of ill repute, murders, and alcohol trafficking through the vaults, the echoing chambers have become quite a haunted place. A few ghostly personalities have made their presence known in some not-so-subtle ways.

The story of how the vaults came into existence actually starts 40,000 years ago during the Ice Age. On the great hill, where Edinburgh Castle stands watch over the city, a volcano once stood. As the rivers of glacial ice encountered the hardened volcanic rock of the mountain, the glaciers split and went around either side of the great mound, carving deep valleys on both sides and then coming back together again, forming a teardrop-shaped piece of land that escaped glacial erosion. Geologists call this a "crag and tail."

Evidence of the site being a military outpost goes back almost three millennia. Given that there are steep cliffs on three sides and a long sloping hill to the top, the position is highly defendable. A fortress of stone was constructed sometime during the reign of Malcolm III

(1058 to 1093 c.e.). As Edinburgh's population grew, people naturally wanted their homes to be as close to the Castle as possible, for protection. The homes were built very closely to one another, and they covered every piece of climbable land surrounding the Castle. In the late 18th century, it was decided that two great bridges would be constructed to span the deep valleys on both sides of the old town of Edinburgh. The first bridge was erected over the northern valley in 1772 and called the North Bridge. In 1785, an even longer southern bridge, with 19 arches supporting the road, was built to span the ravine of the Cowgate; it was named the South Bridge. Both bridges connected Edinburgh to new, level land, where grid street systems could be laid out to accommodate the population growth of the city.

On either side of the bridges, tenement buildings were constructed immediately adjacent to the bridge. With buildings on either side, the arches would be enclosed, forming the Edinburgh vaults. The tenements were so predominant they almost entirely masked the bridge.

Photo courtesy of Mercat Tours.

Des Brogan is one of the founders of Mercat Tours and coauthor of the book *Hidden and Haunted: Underground Edinburgh*. Brogan, a former history teacher in Edinburgh, spoke to me about the underground vaults. He said, "By the middle of the 19th century, these vaulted areas were being used as workshops by many of the people who lived in the tenements." By 1790, cobblers, butchers, wine merchants, bookbinders, jewelers, and many other businesses all stood on South Bridge selling their services and wares. One level below, these merchants had their workshops, and another floor below that were living quarters and cooler storage. "People just got on with their business in those kind of dark, dank areas," Brogan said. But the construction of the bridge wasn't watertight.

Over the decades, the Scottish rain leaked through the bridge into the lowest parts of the vaults, spreading illness and death. As prosperity grew for the merchants who lived and worked on the South Bridge, many were able to move their living quarters to better housing. Those who couldn't afford to move found themselves in what was fast becoming a slum. By the 1840s, the city council resolved to remove all of the legal residents, which meant the caverns would become a haven for the poverty-stricken and the underbelly of Edinburgh.

During the Irish potato famine of 1845–1847, the destitute Irish came over to Scotland in droves. They had no money, no employment, and very few prospects, so they settled in the vaults. Prostitution, whiskey stills, gambling, fights, and murders were all taking place in the vaults in the latter half of the 19th century. By the early 20th century, the vaults were sealed off, eliminating the refuge of Edinburgh's dark side.

In the 1980s, the vaults were rediscovered by former rugby international star Norrie Rowan, who owns some property that includes a section of the vaults. Rowan crawled through an opening and discovered part of an underground city.

At Rowan's invitation, and after some cleanup and electric light installation, Mercat Tours began offering historic walks through the vaults. But they found more than just some great history. "The more people we took down there, the more things began to happen," Brogan said. "If they [people on the tour] were at all sensitive to the other world, they would feel very uncomfortable. On one occasion, we took somebody down who later told us she was a medium, and she identified a number of ghosts that she had seen down there. She was able to give information on what they looked like, whether they were male or female, children or whatever. With that, we took down what she said and subsequently other people and other mediums identified the same characters. These mediums had never met before, and we had never published anything, so there was no way that they could've colluded or made it up. It struck us then that we were in possession of a tremendous amount of information that was being added to all the time from people all over the world. It was giving us a fairly accurate picture of the paranormal within the vaults."

The accounts of ghost encounters continued to accumulate over the years. The stories reinforced each other, and many people were seeing different aspects of the same characters. The ghosts of birds and even a shaggy dog plopping itself down at visitors' feet has been reported in addition to the human spirits. A few of these human spirits definitely stand out.

"Jack" is the ghost of a little boy reported to be in late 18th-century dress and wandering the arches. "We think he was killed during the construction of the bridge, and his spirit is still within the confines of the vaults," Brogan said. "There are a number of [spirits of] children who run around. Our customers who go down there have felt the hand of a child put into their hand as they're standing there. Or they'll hear the laughter of the kids."

The darkest and most notorious presence in the vaults is that of Mr. Boots. If someone seems intentionally frightened, or if a psychically sensitive person feels threatened, it's attributed to Mr. Boots. "We call him that because he wears knee-length boots, very rough trousers that fit into the boots, and a very dirty ruffled white shirt," Brogan said. "He's unkempt and unshaven, and he has very bad breath. We know this because people can smell it. If our guide is telling stories, he will appear behind the group. And only some people in the group will see him. But as soon as he's spotted, he disappears."

Mr. Boots seems particularly connected to one room of the vaults. Several of the mediums who have investigated Mr. Boots's room believe it to be a crime scene. Brogan said, "We have lighting in the vaults that is subdued. And we have candlelight, of course, as well. In his room, a light always points to the floor because he has told us [through the mediums] that if the light shines in his face, he'll go berserk. He doesn't like us being there. One of the reasons is that he occupies the room along with a girl that he actually murdered, and the ghost of the girl is still in the room as well."

Brogan believes Mr. Boots feeds off of the energy from the groups of people. On occasion, Mr. Boots has been reported to act out. Brogan said, "On a number of occasions, he has shown his unhappiness by switching off all the lights. There's absolutely no reason why there should be light failure, but the lights all go out. And not only that, the candles go out as well," leaving the guide and the group in complete darkness, entombed in a stone cavern. The guides are careful to fore-warn about Mr. Boots.

Brogan has never seen Mr. Boots, but he has heard him. "He stomps along the various corridors in the vaults, and you can hear him walking." Brogan has also reported feeling drastic temperature changes between different rooms of the vault. He said, "Because it's beneath the streets, and because the tenement buildings are still there, there's a very ambient temperature. No matter what the temperature is like outside, it was always the same downstairs. And yet there are times that I've been down there, and as I went from one room to another, the room ahead is freezing cold. There's absolutely no way that that could happen. But it's there."

Considering the area of the underground vaults, at its peak population, it's likely that several hundred people lived there. Over the roughly 130-year history of the vaults being inhabited, it's likely there were more than 100 deaths—most died of sickness or old age, but there were certainly several murders.

The underground vaults of Edinburgh are a place where the poorest of the poor sought shelter. Against all adversity—disease, crime, and no employment—some of the denizens of the vaults would prevail to a better way of life. Sadly, some not only made the vaults their home, but their tomb as well, and these poor souls may never leave.

Photo courtesy of Mercat Tours.

Chapter 21:
THE PIRATES' HOUSE

The Pirates' House is located one block from the Savannah River, in the most historic section of Savannah, Georgia. Dinner is served daily from 5:30 p.m. Photo by Gennie Bailey.

THE PIRATES' HOUSE:

Savannah, Georgia

Tel: 1 (912) 233-1881

Web: *www.thepirateshouse.com*

TOP SECRET

Have you heard of Captain Flint?

"Heard of him, you say! He was the bloodthirstiest buccaneer that sailed. Blackbeard was a child [compared] to Flint. The Spaniards were so prodigiously afraid of him that, I tell you, sir, I was sometimes proud he was an Englishman," was Squire Trelawney's reply to that very question asked in Robert Louis Stevenson's classic tale *Treasure Island*.

Robert Louis Stevenson based all of the characters in *Treasure Island* on real people and infamous pirates. The notorious Flint was no exception.

Stevenson was a writer who did his homework. Though *Treasure Island* was first published in book form in 1883, Stevenson captured the names, boats, places, and mood of the pirates' heyday, which took place about 150 years prior. Reportedly, while Stevenson was in Savannah, he stepped into a tavern and heard the story of a feared, blue-faced drunkard of a pirate captain, who died in one of the inn's rooms, still calling for more rum. "Fetch aft the rum, Darby!" were Captain Flint's last words to Darby M'Graw as Stevenson reported them in *Treasure Island*.

It's possible that back in the late 1870s, Stevenson also heard that this scoundrel's ghost still haunted the tavern. The pirate's tenacious attitude of refusing to follow the rules, even in death, may have inspired Stevenson to write this passage about Flint: "Dead—aye, sure enough he's dead and gone below… but if ever sperrit walked, it would be Flint's."

That infamous pub still stands today, though you won't find buccaneers any longer—with the exception of one ghostly pirate captain who still haunts the building. The locals have taken to calling this ghost "Flint" for lack of knowing his real name, and for believing this person was the inspiration for the character. Today, the tavern is an upscale restaurant called, appropriately enough, the Pirates' House.

The story of the Pirates' House starts with the founding of Savannah in 1733, as colonists arrived from England. A tent city was erected and a large experimental garden was planted. Botanists brought vines, seeds, flowers, and herbs from around the world to the 10-acre plot. The colonists needed to know what would grow in the area and what would not—high hopes were placed on grape vines for winemaking and mulberry trees for culturing silk. Neither took to the climate and soil, but they did discover peach trees fared very well. After 20 years, Georgia's growing cycles were established, Savannah was turning into a beautiful seaport town, and the great garden wasn't necessary anymore.

The Pirates' House was originally built by seamen in 1754. The construction was wooden beams, interlocked and held together by wooden pegs—the way seamen built ships. The construction in this section of town stands in contrast to the well-built, Colonial-style homes in the center of town.

The Pirates' House was a dangerous place, full of swashbuckling pirates and scallywags. Seamen would stop in for grog and rum as they arrived from ports around the world. With the exception of the pirate Jean Pierre Lafitte, who married a woman from the same neighborhood and came from a later era, it's difficult to place the names of too many famous pirates who actually visited this early tavern.

A pirate's life for you, you say? I spoke with Robert Edgerly, a life-long Savannah native and pirate expert who runs Savannah Walking Tours, which features a historical tour called the Pirate's Walk. Edgerly said, "Pirates lived short lives, and they didn't care. When you think about a seaman's life, these guys had it made, compared to the average seaman. So they didn't care if they had a short life and if they hung at the end of a rope at the age of 40, because they had seen much more than anybody else had ever seen."

Edgerly explained how many infamous pirates, such as Blackbeard, Calico Jack, and Stede Bonnet, all came through the area of Savannah, but decades before the English ever settled there and long before the Pirates' House became a rough and tough sailor's pub.

In the Pirates' House rum cellar, there was a tunnel connecting the building to the Savannah River—a drunken (or sometimes drugged) sailor could pass out in the corner of the pub and awake the next day on an unfamiliar ship at sea. Pirate captains were notorious for kidnapping crew if they were short-handed. Edgerly said, "Ships that sailed had to have so many men on them or they were unseaworthy. If the ship was loaded and ready to go and they didn't have enough men, they sent out a press gang. There was one ponytailed marine for authority and about six or eight big guys. Back in that era in a seaport, you didn't walk around alone because of the press gangs. They weren't looking for old guys, they weren't looking for lame guys—they were looking for able-bodied, young fellows. And the local authorities would turn a blind eye to it unless he was married, had children, or was from a family of wealth. They would turn a blind eye because it was good for commerce."

Edgerly explained that sailors pressed into service wouldn't be let off the ships when they arrived at different seaports around the world because of fear they would run off. But press gangs weren't the only way to kidnap a sailor. Edgerly said, "If the press gangs couldn't find anybody, then they'd go to the area that is now called the Pirates' House and they'd find an able-bodied seaman who already had experience, who had a little too much grog, or they'd hasten his lethargy with a knockout shot to the head. We know that the basement of the captain's quarters—the 1750 Cypress Building—is a rum cellar. They'd go down there, and during the day there would be men tied and shackled around the kegs of rum, and then that night they'd drag them through the tunnels and out to sea."

With a record of abducted seamen, hardened pirates drinking themselves to death, and more than 250 years of American history, the Pirates' House has more than its share of ghost stories. I also spoke with Greg Profitt, who runs Savannah By Foot, a walking tour company that features the "Creepy Crawl Haunted Pub Tour." Profitt's Boston accent immediately gives away that he wasn't raised in Savanna—an obstacle Profitt would have to overcome to win over the locals who at first treated him as a carpetbagger. Profitt arrived in Savannah in April of 1990 as a skeptic, but he would become a believer when he started his Creepy Crawl a few years later. He and his tourist guests have had several profound ghostly experiences in the Pirates' House.

Profitt said, "I'd start my tours at the Pirates' House. Upstairs there was a lounge called Hannah's East. I remember one night I had a lot of people in there, and I'm going around to the tables and I'm saying to people we're going to be leaving in a few minutes, if you could finish your drink or grab a to-go cup. There were two sisters from Atlanta and they both had their glasses almost empty. They were going to go up to the bar and get one more and then leave, because you can carry your drink around with you in Savannah. All of a sudden, as I turned to walk away, this woman screams. I turned back and her drink glass is absolutely stuffed with Spanish moss. She was just totally freaked out."

On another occasion, Profitt was speaking with a young couple from Atlanta at the start of his tour at the Pirates' House bar. Profitt said, "They said to me, 'Before we get going, is any of this real?' And right across from us beside the cash register on the other side of the bar there was a stack of glasses in a pyramid shape. They didn't fall down, they exploded. Literally exploded—glass went everywhere. And the customer said, 'Never mind.'"

Profitt has done a lot of work with charity in Savannah over the years. In fact, it would be a dare between friends that would lead Profitt to an overnight stay in the Captain's Room dining room—the most haunted part of the restaurant. Tony Cross, a fundraiser for Savannah's Leukemia Society, bet Greg Profitt $200 that he wouldn't last overnight inside the Pirates' House. Profitt said he would take the dare if Cross joined him. The idea turned into a charity event where people sponsored the two men in this ghost-a-thon. Profitt and Cross raised over $6,000 for the leukemia foundation and, in the process, had more of a ghostly experience than they bargained for.

Profitt said, "It was really bizarre; we heard a lot of noises. We were the only ones in the building, and we were supposed to stay up in the one room, but I roamed all through the place—I couldn't help it; it was fascinating. We kept hearing footsteps and banging on the walls and banging on doors, and we're investigating but we're finding nothing. Tony was up there to kind of keep me honest—he didn't believe in ghosts. He's this British guy, and at about a quarter 'til 1, he's reading from the book *Treasure Island* and he reads, 'Darby, bring me more rum.' He threw on a lot of accent, almost like he was reading to a crowd. I had brought Jamaican rum, because in the book Flint's last words were, 'Fetch aft the rum, Darby!'

"Well I brought rum and three shot glasses. I had mine, Tony had his, and the third one was in a position where either one of us, to get near it, would have to get up to move to it. At a quarter 'til 1, when he reads, 'Darby, bring me more rum' out of the book, that one shot glass that neither one of us could have reached, it just vanished with the rum in it. We watched it disappear."

Profitt isn't the only witness to the supernatural at the Pirates' House, by any means. Robert Edgerly said, "I know people who have actually seen the ghost of the big, burly fellow sitting at the table. Because the Pirates' House has been there so long, there are generations of people that have worked there. And I've talked to credible individuals—I mean guys that wouldn't give it a second thought—that have seen the ghost. The restaurant used to be 20 dining rooms, but now the 45 South [an adjacent restaurant] has taken over some of it. There's like 14 dining rooms, and the reason being is that some of them are the old living rooms, bedrooms of the houses that were adjacent. I've had at least three managers tell me over a 20-year period that they would be walking through there at night closing up, they'd go by a room and they'd look, and there would be a guy there at the table. They'd go back and look again, and he'd look at them. Then they'd get scared to death, go get somebody, and bring them back, and there wouldn't be anybody there. People have seen the old ship captain, whoever he is, sitting there."

When Greg Profitt was sharing some of his ghostly experiences with author Frances Kermeen at the Pirates' House bar, both experienced a threatening phenomenon when the author was typing notes into her laptop. Profitt said, "As soon as we started talking about the ghost, her laptop computer goes wacko. It starts spitting out numbers, letters, and symbols—you really couldn't understand what it was, the keys were going on their own, and it crashed. She reboots the computer, and this time it was like words. They were kind of running in together: *hate, die*. And the third time, it really seemed to be threats against me—that I should shut up, discontinue, or bad things were going to happen to me."

The spirit of Flint in all of his menacing glory still walks the Pirates' House. Other witnesses have heard ghostly cries for rum, and some have seen the sea captain himself. If you go there, matey, buy him some rum or grog, and don't let your guard down—you don't want to wake up at sea, pressed into the service of Captain Flint.

Chapter 22:
BOGGO ROAD GAOL MUSEUM

Boggo Road Gaol Museum is open for tours Monday through Friday, 9 a.m. to 3 p.m., and is also available to accommodate private functions. Additionally, Ghost Tours of Brisbane makes regular stops at Boggo Road as part of their tour. Photo by Matthew Meier.

BOGGO ROAD GAOL MUSEUM:

Brisbane, Queensland

Tel: 61 (07) 3846-7423

Web: *www.boggoroadgaol.com.au*

Prisons don't hold fond memories for most people. The dregs of society are housed in these correctional houses. Sometimes violent criminals are sentenced to the ultimate punishment at the hangman's gallows, and other prisoners find the cramped quarters and lack of freedom maddening, to the point that they take their own lives. Occasionally, the honest citizens who work as prison guards fall victim themselves, in a riot or when a desperate inmate gets the upper hand. It's a small wonder why jails are often home to supernatural occurrences. Boggo Road Gaol (jail) in the Queensland city of Brisbane is now a museum that holds relics of Australia's early penal system. Inside, visitors see how the prison worked, its cell blocks, its old furnishings, and on some occasions, the ghosts of its former inmates.

The Boggo Road Gaol site was designated as a penitentiary reserve in 1880. In July of 1883, a prison for men had opened on the land to help ease the overcrowding of Queensland jails. In 1898, the state government deemed that a new women's prison was also necessary, and construction of the new facility began in October 1901. The female division, number two division, opened on October 3, 1903—the first women's prison in Queensland.

Number two division operated as a women's prison until 1921, when the demands for more prison space forced the government to make all of Boggo Road's facilities for men. Boggo Road was a place where many different criminals did time.

John Banks began working as a guard at Boggo Road in 1972. He spoke to me about some of the jail's history and inmates. He said, "If you came in on nonpayment of maintenance, you finished up in here. If you were found drunk on Friday night around Brisbane, you came to these places. It wasn't a selected group that came in here." But Boggo Road also had its notorious inmates.

The prison closed in 1989, and most of Boggo Road's buildings were demolished with the exception of division two. With the help of John Banks and two other former guards, the site became a museum in 1992. More than 20,000 visitors a year pass through the iron gates to see what prison life was like. In addition to tours, the building is also rented out for private functions and film shoots. Banks says they've even had wedding ceremonies and receptions done on the prison grounds.

Photo by Matthew Meier.

"You get married, you do a life sentence," he said. "You might as well do it in jail."

Boggo Road's most well-known inmate is also one of its most notorious. The local lore says this notorious criminal is still around—that he made a deal with the devil. On September 22, 1913, Ernest Austin had the distinction of being the last prisoner hung in all of Queensland before capital punishment was abolished throughout Australia in 1922. Austin was sentenced to death for murdering an 11-year-old girl named Ivy Mitchell, who lived in the Samford section of northern Brisbane. Austin showed no remorse during his trial. When Austin got to the gallows, the official report said he announced his remorse and then was hung without incident. But there's another version—one that may explain why Austin might still be hanging around.

Jack Sim, local Brisbane historian, has been running Brisbane Ghost Tours since 1998. "The papers at the time reported he [Austin] was sorry for what he did," Sim said. "But old-timers here reckon he laughed and said: 'She loved it'—referring to his victim—'she enjoyed it'—referring to the terrible act he perpetrated upon her—and 'I would do it again if I could.'

"As the executioner released the trapdoors beneath his feet, the murderer began to laugh, all the way to the very end of the 13-foot rope.

Even then he tried to force out one last little chuckle from between his lips. It was said that the laughter was often heard in the early mornings in the cellblocks."

According to Sim, some of the locals believed part of Austin's agreement with the devil was to gather more souls. This could be part of the reason for many Austin sightings around the prison. Sim said, "Ernest Austin was reported to torment the prisoners and guards for years after his death. The prison has what I would define as a haunted atmosphere. It definitely still has a feeling of human occupation, even though it's been unused as a prison since 1992."

One security feature of the prison was the peastone gravel placed all around the divisions. On quiet evenings it's impossible to walk on the gravel without making a lot of crunching noise. Guards reported seeing darting shadows and other "ghosties" that their sleepy states seemed to induce. There is a long history at Boggo Road of guards avoiding the night shift in all possible ways. "There were some 'screws,' who would not do the night shifts," Sim said. "When they were rostered onto night shifts, they would do anything to swap to a different night. Some of them appear on the rosters of the time, but they maintain that they actually didn't show up; another officer took their place. One officer told me that a mate of his never once in 15 years as a guard here actually did night shift. On his record it says he did, as it does on his timesheets. But, a packet of tobacco slipped to the right person took care of the details."

According to Sim, one documented ghost encounter occurred in 1970 when a prison officer saw what he referred to as a "big, white, shapeless mass" on top of the dividing wall of the exercise yard in the old number one division. This was in the early hours of the morning— the officer claimed the white mass slid off the wall and disappeared into the darkness. Sim said, "The spot where he saw the 'ghost' was just behind A Wing, where the gallows used to be. The prison officer asked for a transfer to Townsville Jail. Who could blame him? I'd have transferred from here too if I could have."

Incarceration in Boggo Road jail was cramped. According to Banks, cells were roughly 8 feet by 9 feet, with a bunk bed, single bed, a combination toilet/tub, and three prisoners. These conditions caused stress for both inmates and staff. Banks said, "Prisoners hung themselves. They attempted to commit suicide in other ways too. Some succeeded, some didn't. We had a prison officer killed here in 1966."

Although the exact number of prisoners who died at Boggo Road jail during its 106 years of operation is not exactly known, when you account for executions, suicides, murders, disease, and natural causes, conservative estimates put the number of deaths in excess of 100.

Conditions were so bad at the prison that there were uprisings. From 1974 until 1985, prisoners insighted several riots. Clothing and furniture would be burned. The foam mattresses would be set ablaze until the foam melted into a boiling hot ooze of chemicals. The rioting inmates would fill tins with the hot substance and throw it at the guards. Banks said, "It's most probably as bad as what it would be in the front line of a war. It's a hell of an experience. People yelling and smashing and making noises."

Watching out for the living inmates was not the only thing a Boggo Road guard had to encounter. The first time Banks heard about the ghosts at Boggo Road Gaol was shortly after he started working there in the 1970s. "We had officers here you'd have to relieve at 2:00 in the morning because they just didn't want to be here," Banks said. "They'd turn around and be white as a sheet and say, 'I've seen a ghost.' So you'd move him away from here and put him somewhere else. We've had officers here that have seen ghosts walk around. They'll see a person walk by and they know quite well they're the only one here."

The guard killed in 1966 has been spotted in the jail by guards and visitors alike. I'm withholding the fallen guard's name, as his widow and children still live in the area. Sim has spotted a specter on his ghost tours at Boggo Road. He said, "I've seen the ghost of a prison officer walking the grounds of number two division; there's no doubt."

Photo by Matthew Meier.

Matthew Meier is a Brisbane-based ghost hunter who first heard about the ghost legends at Boggo Road four years ago when he read about the ghost tours there. His first investigation took place March 6, 2004, when he and his wife went for an evening tour. He said, "On more than one occasion, some of the very heavy cell doors on the top floor slammed shut in the cell block that we had set up our video cameras in. And I mean these doors are rusty and very hard to move, so it was not the wind—and it was not windy that night either. I caught the sound of one of the doors shutting on camera; not proof, but still interesting. You get the feeling of being watched constantly there."

Meier isn't the only one to hear the slamming cell doors. Banks claims he's never seen a ghost. However, "Funny things do happen around here. We have noises in the place we cannot explain," Banks said. "It'll sound like a bolt slamming on a door, or sound like a door being closed. Other officers would hear people walking around on gravel and go down to inspect and there's no one there."

Some of the prisoners at Boggo Road Gaol appear to have an eternal life sentence. The old buildings, cells, and furniture speak to passersby of a rigid lifestyle where some prisoners were forced into submission, others into madness and suicide, and some were lucky enough to get out and on with their lives.

Chapter 23:
STONE'S PUBLIC HOUSE

Stone's Public House is a bar and restaurant that serves lunch and dinner Tuesday through Sunday. Photo by Jeff Belanger.

STONE'S PUBLIC HOUSE:

Ashland, Massachusetts

Tel: 1 (508) 881-1778

Web: *www.stonespublichouse.com*

Stone's Public House was originally built in 1832 and is well-known today for its charming, old New England décor, its food, and its spirits—and not necessarily the kind you drink. Located next to the Boston & Albany railroad tracks and at the heart of Main Street in Ashland, Massachusetts, the restaurant no longer takes overnight guests. Well, not the living kind, anyway.

In 1832, Captain John Stone, a wealthy landowner who heard the railroad was going to come through town, decided to build an inn near the Ashland Rail Station to capitalize on the new traffic that would be coming to and through Ashland. Originally called "The Railroad Boarding House," John Stone personally ran the inn for only a few years. He would eventually sell the establishment to his brother, Napoleon. During the early days of the railroad and of the inn, many famous faces stopped by—Daniel Webster even gave a speech from the balcony.

The establishment changed owners many times throughout its history. It would be renamed the "Ashland Hotel" by one owner, and in 1976, Leonard "Cappy" Fournier bought the Ashland Hotel and renamed it John Stone's Inn after its original owner. This trend of keeping Stone's name out front continues with the current owner, who made a slight alteration to the name to drop the "inn" part of the previous name. Fournier is also the person credited with being the first to explore the ghosts there.

189

In the mid-1980s, Fournier allowed psychics to visit the inn. Ralph Bibbo, founder of Education Concerning a Higher Order (ECHO), reported that there are several ghosts who haunt the inn. Through his communication sessions, Bibbo believes that, around 1845, John Stone, four or five Ashland locals, and a salesman from New York named "Michael" were playing poker. Folklore says the card game turned ugly when the salesman was accused of cheating, and Stone hit him over the head with the butt of his gun with the intent of knocking him out. Unfortunately, the blow killed the salesman, and the group swore to secrecy that they would hide the body and never speak of it again. Allegedly, the body was buried in the basement, but several attempts at random digging have yielded nothing.

The second tragedy to take place there was the unfortunate death of a young girl. She was the niece of one of the former employees and was very sick. She eventually died, while being cared for at the inn.

Inside Stone's Public House, you'll find classic, old New England charm: high ceilings, solid wood beams, and several fireplaces to take the chill out of the Massachusetts winters. Over the fireplace in the bar area sits an old photograph of John Stone himself, and behind the bar is a very intriguing recent photograph, taken on a night when a band was performing in the pub section. In the grain and texture of one of the vertical wooden beams, you can very clearly see the image of a man with a big, black mustache, dressed in old-fashioned clothes.

In the basement of the restaurant, one needs to duck to walk around—you will also need to dodge the many cobwebs. Along the walls are the rocks that make up the original foundation, the old wooden beams that the building rested upon, and in the far corner sits a very interesting bit of history. Several years ago, sewer pipes were being run to the basement of the building, and the workers broke through the cement wall expecting to find solid ground. Instead they found a hidden room.

The hidden room was a rest stop on the Underground Railroad— a series of safe houses, tunnels, and hiding places to smuggle slaves out of the South. The Underground Railroad's activity peaked in the period from the 1830s to the 1860s. "They [the workers] found a cot, a water barrel, and some old blankets [in the room]," said Marti Northover, who owned the establishment until February of 2003.

In the bar room, bartender Jim Terlemezian can tell you about the many ghost stories he has heard—and some he experienced.

"I definitely believe in ghosts, without a doubt," said Terlemezian, who has worked at Stone's Public House since 2001. He recounted an experience he had in 2002: "We came in on a Sunday to work a function, so I got in around 10 a.m. and worked until about 2 a.m., so I was exhausted. Everybody had cleared out, and it was just me and Marti [Northover]. She was upstairs in her office, and I was on the first floor at the end of the bar. I went to the back to change my shirt and left the door open. As I take my shirt off, I hear a voice. I can't tell you what they said—I couldn't even tell you if it was a male or a female, but it was a young kid.

"I stopped what I was doing and came out [to the main bar] and said, 'Marti?' I thought maybe she said 'Jim' or something like that. But she wasn't even here; she was upstairs. So I went back and continued to put my shirt on, and I heard another voice. It was an older voice—I was pretty positive it was a woman. I don't know of any women spirits who are in this place, [but] there again it was one word, and I couldn't tell you what it was. I heard two different voices on that day."

It seems as though just about all of the staff has had some supernatural experience at the restaurant. Scott Campbell, part of the kitchen staff, who has also worked there since 2001, spoke of two of his experiences in November 2002: "There was a glass bottle of malt vinegar on top of the fridge. There was no one over there [by the refrigerator], and three of us were on the side of the kitchen. All of a sudden we heard a large crash. We were surprised and didn't know what was going on, so we go over there and we see a bottle of malt vinegar on the ground. We said, 'What the heck, you mean it's not broken?' Something that fell 6 feet to the ground should have definitely broken—it wasn't very thick glass.

"Another time, someone tapped me on the back, I turned around, and no one was there."

One of the more haunting stories involves a dress that is stored at the inn. Terlemezian explained, "Supposedly there is a dress upstairs, on the third floor, with blood stains on it. There was an old waitress/manager who worked here, and she brought her boyfriend and went up to the third floor, took the dress, and brought it out of here and had it in her trunk. She had a lot of strange things happen to her, so she gave it to her boyfriend to hold, and he also experienced strange events—like being woken up in the middle of the night by strange sounds and voices."

Northover continued the story: "She [the waitress] came to me and told me, 'Look, this is what I did, and I have to bring the stuff back here because at home all hell broke loose.' She swears she heard noises, furniture moving, and she was freaked out even driving with the dress in the car."

Northover and the waitress brought the dress back to its rightful place on the third floor, where it allegedly still lies today.

When asked if she was a believer in the supernatural, Northover replied, "I am now. There are at least seven spirits in this place." She believes these spirits are those of John Stone; the murdered New York salesman; the young girl; a manager who died about 20 years ago, after being hit by a train, while trying to push a car off the tracks; and possibly some slaves who never made it to freedom.

Some of the patrons have also seen some unexplained things. Northover said, "There was a woman here one night, and she sat at the table in the corner and called the waitress over and told her, 'Do you realize there are three spirits in here right now? There is an old woman sitting down and waiting for someone. There is a man smoking a pipe pacing up and down, and there is another man.' We smell pipe smoke all of the time—I even smelled it yesterday."

Photo by Jeff Belanger.

In February of 2003, Matt Murphy took ownership of John Stone's Inn and renamed it Stone's Public House—the renaming was due to the fact that the restaurant hasn't taken overnight guests in many decades and people were calling from around the country wishing to stay in the haunted inn. Murphy says he was aware of the ghost stories before buying the restaurant. Stone's Public House was closed from February to June of 2003, while Murphy did some renovations to the kitchen and second-floor dining rooms. He said, "Everybody warned us that, once we started the construction, we were going to open the floodgates. Nothing happened, so we surmised that they [the ghosts] actually liked the work we did. We did some cosmetic work, especially upstairs. We did want to keep it in the spirit—no pun intended—of the period."

Though Murphy hasn't personally seen any supernatural activity, the ghost stories do continue. He said, "Two instances that actually copied each other happened when people were leaving. They looked behind them and saw a little girl in the second-floor window." Murphy's staff also has their feelings on the hauntings. Murphy said, "The manager comes in and she's heard a lot of noises upstairs as if somebody's up there. And she won't go up there. At the same time, she's not going to leave the building. She's kind of like, 'So what, as long as they stay up there.'"

Stone's Public House is a veritable hotbed of supernatural activity. Staff, customers, and passersby all have their own ghost stories to share about this quaint New England restaurant. But remember, if you come for dinner, you may actually be dining with John Stone himself, so be sure to give him a toast.

Chapter 24:
MUNCASTER CASTLE

Muncaster Castle has accommodations for 18, in addition to the featured "ghost sit," where a group of guests can rent out the haunted Tapestry Room of the castle for their own investigations. Located in Cumbria, the Lake District of England, the castle also offers tours and banquet facilities. Photo courtesy of Muncaster Castle.

MUNCASTER CASTLE:

Ravenglass, England

Tel: 44 (0) 1229-717-614
Web: *www.muncaster.co.uk*

TOP SECRET

With ghostly encounters, we often expect to find the opening and closing of doors by unseen forces, strange sounds and smells coming from thin air, pranks, and other general tomfoolery. And if ever there were a place for ghostly tomfoolery, Muncaster Castle would be it. Located in northwestern England and built around 1258 C.E., the castle has been home to the Pennington family for almost 800 years. It was at Muncaster Castle that Thomas Skelton, better know as "Tom Fool," served as court jester, as well as tutor for the Pennington children, during the latter half of the 16th century. But Tom Fool is not the only ghost said to be haunting the Castle. Tom gets the credit for the pranks, but other entities get the credit for the cries and scares.

In 1208 C.E., 23,000 acres of land were granted to Alan de Penitone. Gamel de Mulcastre, 50 years later, built Muncaster Castle on this vast expanse in West Cumberland, by the River Esk. Muncaster Castle played a significant role in English history—it served as a stronghold to repel marauding Scots from the north, it was an outpost to protect trade routes from Carlisle, and it was home to the Pennington family— a family of great influence in the region. One famous guest of the Castle included King Henry VI; in 1464, Sir John Pennington gave shelter to the King when he was found wandering after the Battle of Hexham. As a token of his appreciation, the King left a drinking bowl and declared that as long as the bowl remained wholly unbroken, the

Penningtons would live and thrive in the Castle. Today, the bowl is still intact and is known around the Castle as the "Luck of Muncaster."

Peter Frost-Pennington has been living at the Castle since 1987. Today, he lives on the now 1,800-acre estate with his wife and three children. The family oversees the guest accommodations, the facilities, and the grounds that receive more than 70,000 visitors per year. I spoke with Frost-Pennington about his experiences with his ghostly tenants. He said, "There have always been the ghost stories about Muncaster, and at least initially, we didn't really talk about them outside the family at all."

Frost-Pennington claims that he and his family have yet to experience any of the ghosts personally, but he certainly doesn't discount all of the personal accounts he's heard from his guests.

Tom Fool's influence can be felt all around the Castle. In fact, poor Tom is now the scapegoat for anything that goes wrong there, but it's all in good fun, Frost-Pennington said.

Thomas Skelton, though he played the fool, was actually quite a clever man and renowned enough that his name was added to the English lexicon. (We can thank this infamous character for the term *tomfoolery*.) He was the kind of servant who saw himself as an equal to his master. Tom Fool used his humor and wit to get away with antics that would have landed someone else's head on the chopping block.

There's an old chestnut tree at Muncaster that Tom Fool took a fancy to sitting under. He spoke with passersby who asked for directions, and he decided in an instant if he liked them or not. If he liked them, Fool would point the travelers in the right direction to London. If he didn't like them, he'd point the unsuspecting voyagers toward quicksand and swamps. A sadistic man for sure, it was a gruesome deed he performed for his master, Sir Ferdinand Pennington, that would make his legend dark.

Apparently, a local carpenter named Dick took a fancy to Sir Pennington's daughter. By Pennington's orders, Tom Fool was to decapitate the carpenter with his own hammer and chisel, and Tom was happy to do it because he believed Dick had weezend (shrunken) three shillings, which he had hidden in a hole, into three pennies. According to William Armistead's 1891 work "The Ill-fated Lovers," after Tom carried out the murderous deed, he said, "I have hid Dick's head under a heap of shavings; and he will not find that so easily, when he awakes, as he did my shillings."

Frost-Pennington told me about a strange encounter that the staff at the Castle attributes to Tom Fool. He said, "People have often complained about door handles turning and there's no one there—as if somebody's trying to get in a room or holding the door against you. I must admit I didn't really believe that. I thought it was people just making it up until, within the last year, a member of staff, who has worked for me for eight years now, got very scared in a part of the Castle. No one knew she was going there; it was a locked room. Well, she fled because she was putting her hand out to open the door, and the door handle started turning. And she thought she was imagining it, and she put her hand back and it was indeed turning. She just fled. She had the only key for that lock—she doesn't go into that part of the Castle at all anymore. The only explanation I have is if you stand on the other side of the door and turn the handle, it turns the handle on the other side. So in other words, someone must have been in that room turning the handle. But no one could have been in that room because it's a locked cupboard. There's no other way in, and no one knew that she was going there."

The Muncaster Castle staff and guests still take Tom Fool's spirit seriously enough to make offerings to him. Dr. Jason Braithwaite, who has been studying the ghost legends of Muncaster since 1990, said, "We do our best to keep him happy where his portrait is hanging. Occasionally, we leave him a little glass of whiskey by the table. If we're having a dinner party at the Castle, Peter will often set a place at the table for Tom, an empty place, and he won't forget to give him a drink of wine. Little traditions like that you wouldn't dare forget to do it. We're still living with Tom Fool in many ways. I think that Tom would be very pleased to know that people are still talking about him up at Muncaster, and that he still is very much a part of the community."

One hot spot of ghostly activity at Muncaster is the Tapestry Room. Until the mid-1990s, the Tapestry Room bedroom was part of the main castle and was not used as part of the accommodations the Castle rents. Personal guests of the family were invited to stay there during their visits, but the practice was short-lived. Frost-Pennington said, "We had friends of the family coming to stay, and we had to stop putting them in the Tapestry Room because it was so embarrassing. They would come down in the morning and we'd say, 'Did you sleep well?' And they'd say, 'No, I had a bloody awful night.' So the only people who stay in that room now are the ghost hunters." The room's guests complained of hearing a baby's cry go on and on throughout the night, keeping them awake.

Frost-Pennington's research shows him that the Tapestry Room was once used as a nursery in the 1860s. Today Muncaster offers a package they call a "ghost sit," where those brave enough can rent out the Tapestry Room for the evening.

Photo courtesy of Muncaster Castle.

Muncaster Castle may possibly be the longest ongoing scientific exploration of a haunting in modern times. Dr. Jason Braithwaite of the Association for the Scientific Study of Anomalous Phenomena, based in the United Kingdom, came to Muncaster to try and explain what was causing the ghostly phenomena at Muncaster. Braithwaite is a behavioral psychologist and research fellow at the University of Birmingham in England, and he visits the Castle six or seven times a year to conduct experiments and interview the staff and guests. Braithwaite told me he has spent many nights in the Tapestry Room and has never personally experienced anything supernatural at the Castle, but he admits the goings-on there are pushing his skepticism to its limits. When Braithwaite first began to research the ghostly happenings at Muncaster, no one except the Pennington family and some of the staff knew anything about the ghosts. This meant that if someone did experience supernatural phenomena, they were not influenced by what they had seen or read about the Castle's ghosts.

Around 1995, television programs on haunted locations started to include Muncaster, and in just a few years, they garnered an international reputation for being haunted.

Braithwaite said, "There are about eight instances of what I call the full-blown Tapestry Room experience of at least an hour to three hours of children crying in the room...really tangible experiences that I've documented from eyewitnesses, spanning from the 1940s and 50s into the late 80s. Experiences of the children crying have happened since then, but once you go public with it, how much weight do you put on the more recent accounts?"

No self-respecting English castle would be complete without some accounts of a White Lady. Muncaster's White Lady stems from the story of Mary Bragg. In 1805, Bragg was a housekeeper in Ravenglass and was in love with the footman at Muncaster. But Mary had competition. One of the housemaids was also in love with the footman. One night, two men went to Mary Bragg's residence and summoned her, saying her lover was seriously ill and they would take her to his bedside. Instead, they brutally murdered her by the road to Muncaster. Her body was found, weeks later, floating in the River Esk. Mary Bragg has since been spotted around the Castle grounds.

Frost-Pennington said, "She's not ever seen in the building, but she's this white lady who appears on the main roads around Muncaster and sometimes in the garden. Some people have even reported that they thought they'd hit someone. They were driving on the road, and this figure in white jumps out in front of them—they hit this young girl in front of them. They stopped the car and there's nothing to be seen.

"People have often seen a darting figure, or sometimes she's a solid figure that looks like you or me. Other times, she's just a sort of miasma or mist, but a fairly thick mist. And we do get sort of odd clumps of mist hanging around hills here on occasion, but people I've talked to are sure it wasn't just a bit of the mist. They say, 'Oh, no. It wasn't like that at all. It was different—it was a definite blob.'"

There are also strange encounters that don't fit into the standard Tom Fool, crying baby, or White Lady mold. Frost-Pennington explained that a woman, who was a partner of one of the Muncaster staff members, walked in one day and asked what they were filming that day—because she had just passed what she believed was an actor dressed in a 15th-century costume. It was not that unusual to spot someone walking around in old dress, because there is a lot of filming that goes on at Muncaster, but on this day, there was nothing by way of festivals or filming going on. Frost-Pennington said, "She'd walked down this alleyway in the middle of the day, and this guy apparently walked past her in hose and doublet, and she said hello to him and he didn't say a word. Normally, when you say hello to somebody, they'll say hello back. And she thought that was a bit odd. She turned around thinking about it after a few more steps and turned around to look at him, and he'd gone. She thought he'd just gone through a doorway into this other yard, but when she heard there was definitely no one dressed up in the place that we knew of, what was it that she saw?"

Tom Fool, Mary Bragg, crying babies, darting shadows, and full-bodied apparitions make Muncaster Castle a ghost hunter's paradise. The grand old castle, set on its vast acreage, gives the ghosts and guests plenty of room to wander. But beware of taking directions from any court jesters whom you may encounter sitting beneath a tree—Tom Fool is not to be trifled with.

Chapter 25:
THE ANDREW BAYNE
MEMORIAL LIBRARY

The Andrew Bayne Memorial Library is located in the Bellevue section of Pittsburgh, Pennsylvania. It is open seven days a week. Though no formal tours are offered, visitors are free to walk through the library and explore its paintings, history, and resources. Photo by Jeff Belanger.

THE ANDREW BAYNE
MEMORIAL LIBRARY:

Pittsburgh, Pennsylvania

Tel: 1 (412) 766-7447

Web: *www.einpgh.org/ein/andbayne/*

For decades, there have been sporadic accounts of the ghostly presence of a woman in the Andrew Bayne Memorial Library. Former tenants and staff at the library have reported beeping sounds, footsteps, and the feeling of a spirit's presence. But in the final years of the 20th century, as a giant elm tree that stood outside the library for more than three centuries began to deteriorate due to Dutch elm disease and old age, the ghost inside the library began making herself known with greater frequency and in less subtle ways.

The Andrew Bayne Memorial Library is a two-story, Victorian-style mansion with a brick facade and ornate, yellow, wooden trim on its exterior. Inside you will find dark mahogany woodwork, marble fireplaces, floor-to-ceiling windows, more than 14,000 books, and the ghost of Amanda Bayne Balph.

Amanda's ghost has been considered benevolent by all who have encountered her, albeit playful and at times mischievous. I think it's worth noting how her spirit and the spirit of the elm tree on her property had a connection—enough of a connection to spur a tremendous increase in supernatural activity when the tree's health began to fade.

For more than 300 years, the "Lone Sentinel," a towering 110-foot-tall American elm, stood proudly over the 4-acre lot that is home to the Andrew Bayne Memorial Library and park. In 1983, this great elm was designated as the largest American elm east of the

Mississippi River. But the designation didn't last much longer, as the Dutch Elm blight had afflicted the tree, and its effects are always fatal. The larger the tree, the slower the disease spreads, so it took years for the Lone Sentinel to deteriorate. Throughout the spring and summer of 1998, Bellevue residents, city council members, and arborists all fought to save the ailing tree, but it eventually had to be removed later that year.

The land on which library now stands originally belonged to Andrew Bayne, and his farmhouse stood at what is now the corner of Teece and Balph Avenues. Andrew Bayne was born in Fayette, Pennsylvania, in 1794, and rose to become a well-known figure in Allegheny County. He was a member of the Constitutional Convention of 1837–1838 and served as Sheriff of Allegheny County from 1837 until 1840. He married Mary Anne Mathews of Butler County and brought her back to his farmhouse. They had two daughters—Jane, born in 1844, and Amanda, born in 1846.

In the mid- to late 1800s, land was getting to be a precious commodity as the city of Pittsburgh rapidly expanded. Andrew Bayne divided up his land to give some to each of his daughters, so they could build their own homes there.

In 1870, Amanda married a prominent local architect named James Madison Balph. The couple took advantage of Mr. Bayne's generous offer of land, and James Balph set to work designing and building the stately Victorian mansion in which he and his bride would live. The Balph home was completed in 1875—the same building that would become the future library. In fact, James Balph's initials can still be seen engraved on the glass transom over the front door.

Amanda loved her stately mansion and the great trees surrounding her house. She delighted in her collection of books and the view from the home's big windows. She watched Pittsburgh quickly grow up around her.

In 1880, Amanda's older sister, Jane, married Arthur Teece and took up residence in the house that is now the Lawrence Miller Funeral Home.

Andrew Bayne died in 1881, living to see his two daughters marry and move into their new homes with their husbands. However, neither Amanda nor Jane would ever give their parents any grandchildren, which also meant no heirs to the Bayne property.

Amanda and Jane were generous with their homes and land. The two agreed that the last sister to die would turn the Bayne-Balph home and its property over to the town of Bellevue with the stipulation that the mansion be used as a library for the town and that the acres could not be developed, nor the beautiful elm trees removed—the land was to remain a park for the residents to enjoy. The sisters also threw in a clause that two of the adjacent streets be named in their honor for good measure.

Arthur Teece died in 1884, just four years after his marriage. The widow Jane lived on until 1896. Amanda Bayne Balph was widowed in 1899 and lived out her remaining 13 years alone in the giant house. She had friends, neighbors, and beautiful trees to keep her company until she passed away in August 1912, of natural causes. That same month, the house and land were turned over to the town.

Since 1912, the library has expanded from a collection comprised mostly of Amanda and Jane's personal assortment of books, stored in two rooms of the house, to a much bigger library, with rooms for community meetings. The surrounding property is no longer a field of trees, as many of the elms died off, and jungle gyms, swingsets, sidewalks, and park benches have taken their place.

Before the library expanded enough to fill the entire mansion, the second floor and attic were rented out as apartments. Residents of these apartments have claimed to have supernatural experiences. Millie Albert reported in the October 29, 2003 *Pittsburgh Post-Gazette* that Ted Zettle was one such resident of the library apartments, from 1975 to 1982. Zettle lived there with his wife, Corrie, and eventually his newborn son, Max. Zettle said, "We often heard unaccounted footsteps and a beeping. Incidentally, after our son Max was born, the sounds became much more frequent. It's difficult to explain, but there's a definite friendly presence in the house. We experienced a warm, welcoming feeling there. The house is very elegant, and my guess is that Amanda is happy sharing the home she loves."

Throughout the 1900s, all of the elm trees on the property succumbed to Dutch elm disease—a fungus that has wiped out more than 50 million American elms since the 1930s. The "Lone Sentinel" made it through almost all of the 20th century before it decayed, was pruned, and ultimately taken down for fear that the rotting giant would fall on neighboring buildings. The ghost of Amanda Bayne Balph took notice when the mighty tree was removed.

Sharon Helfrich is director of the Bayne Library and has worked in the building since October of 1998. She said of Amanda's spirit: "She's been around as long as this place has been a library. It's just a case of different sightings here and there. And she seemed to be very active right around the time that our Lone Sentinel was dying. I think it's probably because part of the trust is that no tree in the park is allowed to be touched. Trees and nature and things like that were very important to her, too."

Photo by Jeff Belanger.

As visitors walk around the library's first floor, they may spot a portrait of Andrew Bayne, with his bushy white beard, overlooking the computer room. Near the library's charge desk, over the fireplace, sits a portrait of Amanda Bayne Balph, with a slight, almost Mona Lisa–esque smile. The library staff and patrons know Amanda when they see her.

"I've only seen her once," said Linda Momper, assistant director of the Bayne Library, who worked there since 1993. "I was in the library by myself and was turning on the computers, and I looked up at the window and saw a reflection in there of a woman. I looked behind me and I thought 'Who is in here?' I looked behind me, and nobody was there, and I looked again and saw the reflection again. It looked just like her picture."

Many visitors to the park surrounding the library have reported seeing a woman in the window wearing a large hat when they knew the library was closed. The library staff believes the window above the parking lot was most likely Amanda's bedroom. It's in that particular window that Amanda's ghostly figure is most often spotted. Helfrich said, "We have an alarm system with motion detectors—there's nobody in here that the police wouldn't know about."

Being seen isn't the only way Amanda has made her presence known. She's notorious for playing with light switches, one of the ceiling fans, and even the library's computers. In fact, it was a light-switch prank that made Sharon Helfrich a believer when she first started working at the library. Helfrich was only working evenings at the time. She had turned the lights on in the back office and then went upstairs to put some books away. When she came back down, the lights were turned off, but no one else had access to the back office. She turned the lights back on and went about her business. Had this only happened once, Helfrich may have dismissed the incident as a result of her being absentminded about whether the lights were on or off. However, the same incident would play itself out two more times that same evening. Helfrich would turn the lights on, leave the room, and when she returned, they would be off again.

On another evening, Helfrich was the only person in the library and was getting ready to close, when she discovered the attic light was on. She said, "I actually had to call one of my supervisors at that time because I didn't know where the attic light switch was. I just knew the light was on and hadn't been on before."

On one particularly cold October day, Assumption School first-grade teacher Debbie Scigilano brought 30 of her students to one of the Bayne Library's second-floor rooms for Halloween story time. In the middle of a story, the overhead ceiling fan turned on by itself. The students, Ms. Scigilano, and the library staff took notice. The adults didn't want to alarm the children, so they quickly finished the story, brought the children back out into the main library, and turned the ceiling fan off by its switch. When they returned to the room to get the children's coats, the fan was on again. Some of the library staff believed it was Amanda giving a sign of approval. Though Mrs. Balph never had children of her own, she seems to take some delight in seeing kids in her home.

Other staff members also claim to have heard footsteps, when they knew they were alone in the library. Paula R. Bellin has been working at the library since 2002. She said, "On Saturday mornings, one of us has to come in and open the library—and we don't open until 10:00. One morning I got here, and I know I heard something upstairs—footsteps or something, and I was ready to run out."

Helfrich recounted a story of what happened, in January 2004, to a patron, who pulled into the library parking lot at 8 a.m. on a Saturday, to allow her car to warm up enough to defrost the windows from the cold Pittsburgh winter's day. The library doesn't open until 10 a.m., so this woman knew the building was empty. The witness said she saw the attic light flash on, and then off. This witness then decided she didn't need to wait until the windows were defrosted—she was leaving right then.

Amanda has also taken to playing with the library's computer system. The staff has reported seeing strange numbers occasionally pop up on the computer screen. Helfrich said, "I would be standing at the charge desk computer and then a number would scan on the computer behind me, and no one was anywhere near that computer. I'd hear 'beep,' and a number would come up. We've tried to play some of the numbers she's flashed onto the computer in the lottery, and it never really hits. We love her dearly, but she's not real lucky."

Amanda Bayne Balph is a friendly, albeit lost spirit. Though there were reports of supernatural activity before 1998, it was the loss of the last great elm on the property that spurred Amanda into more frequent activity. The staff of the Bayne Library claims that ghostly activity has calmed down compared to 1998, but occasionally one may still see the generous woman with the big hat peering out of her bedroom window, still looking for the giant elms that once adorned her lawn.

Chapter 26:
THE SPAGHETTI WAREHOUSE

The Spaghetti Warehouse is open 11 a.m. to 10 p.m. Sunday through Thursday, and 11 a.m. to 11 p.m. Friday and Saturday. Ghost tours are offered through an outside company—contact the Spaghetti Warehouse for more details. Photo by Philip Verdieck.

THE SPAGHETTI WAREHOUSE:

Houston, Texas

Tel: 1 (713) 229-9715

Web: *www.meatballs.com*

TOP SECRET

Haunting a place for many decades can build up quite an appetite. It shouldn't come as a surprise that ghosts would want to stick around Houston's Spaghetti Warehouse because the bustling of the staff and customers creates a lot of human energy. However, human energy isn't the only thing The Spaghetti Warehouse spirits feed off of— some have been known to try noshing on the food in the kitchen.

The Spaghetti Warehouse is a national chain of Italian restaurants that has more than 20 locations in nine states. The Houston restaurant, at the corner of Commerce and Travis, is in one of the city's most historic districts. Since 1974, the restaurant has stood in Houston's downtown. The building was built in 1912 and housed the Desel-Boettcher Company, a produce business that stored its perishables in the basement level, had offices on the main floor, and kept nonperishables on the second floor. An elevator ran from the second floor to the basement, for moving products. It is during the time the building sold produce that our ghost story begins.

According to Nikki Hampton, the manager of The Spaghetti Warehouse, the lore that has been passed down tells that, in the 1930s, the manager of Desel-Boettcher was finishing up his workday, when he fell into an elevator shaft and was killed. The folklore says the man's wife reported that he walked into his home that evening, walked down the hallway of the house, and disappeared. When his wife couldn't find him in the house, she became frantic and eventually made her way to the warehouse, where she was told of the accident by other employees at the scene. Oddly enough, the man who fell to his death is not the specter most often reported.

Hampton said, "My boss, the general manager now, about five or six years ago, saw the upper torso of a woman walking through the upstairs dining room. She said she didn't see a head, she didn't see legs or anything, but she could tell it was a woman because it had a bust line. She said she had to do a double take. One second it was there, and the next second it wasn't." The ghost of the woman is most likely a psychic impression caused by the traumatic event years ago when a very distraught wife came to search for her husband who had recently been killed. Many paranormal researchers believe these ghosts are not interactive, the sightings are simply a replay of an event from the past that people occasionally see.

Hampton has worked at The Spaghetti Warehouse since 1987. She had heard some of the ghostly tales, but she didn't believe them until she had her own experience in the summer of 2002, when the general manager of the restaurant sent her to the basement on an errand. Hampton said, "Because this was August, it was really hot downstairs, and the only place we had airconditioning was in our break room. Or if you had the coolers open, you could feel the cool air. I was the only person down there, and none of the coolers were open. I was walking by this area, and it was almost like something cold walked through me. I was standing there, and then all of a sudden I went to walk forward, and it was like something cold just passed through me. It was so bad, it gave me chills. I mean, it was a *dry* cold. It was so cold that I could see my breath in it. It freaked me out. I ran upstairs."

In the spring of 2003, Hampton's staff encountered one of the strangest unexplained events I've ever heard about. Around 11 p.m. one weeknight, Hampton did her walk-through of the restaurant, to make sure everyone had vacated, before she set the alarm and locked up for the evening. After determining everything was normal, she went home. She woke up around 7:30 a.m., when her kitchen manager phoned her after he'd opened the restaurant the following morning. Hampton explained, "He said, 'What's up with the chairs?' I said, 'What are you talking about?' He said, 'Who stacked the chairs up like that? I said, 'What are you talking about?' Because I'm half asleep. He said, 'The chairs are stacked up to the ceiling.'"

The upper dining area of The Spaghetti Warehouse has a ceiling about 14 feet high. In the center of the dining area, the wooden chairs were interlocked within each other, in slight twists, with the leg going through the back of the chair below so the seats fit together almost like puzzle pieces. This went on all the way up to the ceiling. "These are flat-bottomed, heavy, wooden chairs," Hampton said. "It would have taken some time and patience to put these chairs together like that. Something like 80 to 100 chairs were used to make this, because our upstairs seats 120 and most of the chairs were used. I didn't do it. I don't know who did it."

This wasn't the first incident with the chairs upstairs, either. In the late 1990s, the restaurant was having some remodeling work done, and a painting crew came in to do the work after business hours. Because the construction company was licensed and bonded, no manager stayed overnight to supervise. The crew's foreman entered through the back service door of the restaurant and unknowingly locked his crew out of the building, when the door shut behind him. The foreman walked to the upper dining area and went in to use the men's room. When the foreman walked out of the bathroom less than one minute later, every chair at every table in the upstairs dining area had been pulled out from the tables. The foreman got on his walkie-talkie to his crew, asking who the jokers were. The crew informed him they were all locked outside—he was the only person in the entire building. The foreman ran down the stairs and darted out the service door. According to Hampton, that crew immediately left and no longer wanted the job. The project was given to a different painting company.

It's difficult to be inside an Italian restaurant and not feel hungry when the smells of pasta, cheeses, breads, and herbs waft around your nose. Who could blame a ghost for helping himself to a snack in the kitchen? Nikki Hampton was the last to leave one evening and did her inspection of the entire restaurant. She found everything clean and in its place. The next morning was another story. Hampton said, "I came in the next day and saw that somebody was back in the kitchen making sandwiches, and there was a trail of chewed-up debris from one spot to the other. But I'm thinking ghosts can't eat, can they? It was very coincidental that the food looked chewed up, and it was dragging in a trail of several feet, like somebody was trying to walk and eat at the same time."

With such a haunted reputation, ghost hunters were eager to get inside to investigate The Spaghetti Warehouse. I spoke with Pete Haviland, lead investigator for Lone Start Spirits, a paranormal investigative group based in Houston and founded in 1998. Haviland has been studying ghosts since the early 1980s. Lone Star Spirits has conducted eight investigations of The Spaghetti Warehouse since their first visit in 1999. Haviland has photographic evidence of ghosts taken in the restaurant's elevator. "I had two separate pictures, from two different photographers, on two different cameras, months apart, that showed [ectoplasmic] mist in the elevator," he said. Many paranormal researchers believe ghost energy can show up on photographs in the form of spherical balls of energy called *orbs*, or as a smoky, semitranslucent mist called *ectoplasm*.

In October of 2003, Lone Star Spirits was allowed to stay in The Spaghetti Warehouse overnight, in conjunction with a Halloween radio promotion with local radio station 93Q. It was during this overnight expedition that Haviland encountered one of the resident spirits in the upstairs dining room. "I saw a little girl standing in a corner," he said. "There was a picture that was taken, and there was an orb over in the corner, where I was pointing. There were a couple of other people who also noticed there was a darker shadow over in the corner, where I was pointing, about the size of a small girl."

An interesting twist in the haunting of The Spaghetti Warehouse is that several spirits have been encountered in the restaurant, though we only know for sure about the one death in the elevator shaft. There seem to be some spirits attached to something in the restaurant. Both Nikki Hampton and Pete Haviland have their suspicions as to what that object is.

The Spaghetti Warehouse chain has a history of placing local antiques in its restaurants. One such antique in the Houston location is an urn hutch that sits in the second-floor dining room. The hutch is about 4 feet tall, with an urn painted on it. This piece of furniture was used by a family to store the urns that housed the cremated ashes of their loved ones—kind of a portable family cemetery.

Ironically, the place that once stored a family's ashes now holds condiments, salt and pepper shakers, and sugar. Hampton's former boss at The Spaghetti Warehouse told her what he knew of the antiques in the building. Hampton said, "He was telling me that the urn hutch was from a family who ran a plantation. That wouldn't surprise me, because we're in the Houston Cotton Exchange area downtown. He said it was bought from this family, where supposedly the woman had eight or nine kids that all died before the age of 12, from polio, rickets, and other illnesses." Their remains were placed in urns within the hutch.

Haviland's group has a slightly different take on the hutch. Lone Star Spirits boasts among its members doctors, law enforcement agents, researchers, and psychics. Two psychics from Lone Star Spirits independently had similar impressions concerning the urn hutch. Haviland said, "Our psychics told me that there was a little girl that played hide-and-seek in there. She got locked in and she suffocated. One psychic has told me that she has heard the sound of a child crying from the bottom cabinet." If a little girl was still connected to the urn hutch, it could account for some of the sightings and some of the mischief that is attributed to a young girl.

There is also a large, ornate grandfather clock on the main level of the restaurant, which Haviland believes is another hot spot for supernatural activity. "People have reported seeing a little girl standing in front of the clock," he said. "The clock is always cold in front. And something messes with the clock. I've had a psychic tell me that a little girl comes down and plays with that clock."

Many guests of The Spaghetti Warehouse come for the pasta, but stay for the supernatural. Amid its historic setting and antique furnishings, the restaurant is haunted by ghosts with an appetite for games, and occasionally for the food.

Chapter 27:
THE OLDE ANGEL INN

The Olde Angel Inn is an English-style pub and restaurant, with five guest rooms for overnight accommodations. Lunch and dinner are served, and though no formal tours are offered, the staff members are well-versed in the ghost stories there—just ask. Photo courtesy of The Olde Angel Inn.

THE OLDE ANGEL INN:

Niagara-on-the-Lake, Ontario

Tel: 1 (905) 468-3411

Web: *www.angel-inn.com*

Niagara-on-the-Lake is a charming, historic village located almost due south, across Lake Ontario, from Toronto. Though this quaint town is Canadian all the way, one inn flies the British Union Jack flag and not the Canadian Maple Leaf over its main entrance. More than 200 years old, The Olde Angel Inn is one of the region's oldest and most historic buildings. But it doesn't fly the Union Jack just because it's an English pub—the British colors also fly to appease Captain Colin Swayze, the Angel Inn's only permanent guest.

The plaque on the inn's front door says, "Local folklore has it that the Inn is haunted by the ghost of a British Soldier killed at the old Inn during the War of 1812. He is said to walk the Inn's cellars after dark, never visiting the upper floors, so long as a Union Jack flies above the Inn's door."

In 1789, Niagara-on-the-Lake was called Newark, and according to the current owners, on the same site, where the Angel Inn is now, stood a building called The Harmonious Coach House. Newark was on its way to becoming the first capital of Upper Canada, and The Harmonious Coach House played a central role as a place where political and literary figures of the day came to dine. Historical figures such as John Graves Simcoe, the first Lieutenant-Governor; Alexander Mackenzie, the explorer; Prince Edward, the father of Queen Victoria; and Thomas Moore, the Irish national poet, are thought to have spent some time in its restaurant.

The Coach House was located on the same block as the Government House, which was home to senior military officers such as Major-General Sir Isaac Brock. In fact, Brock's aide, John Macdonnell, reportedly died in the house, in agony from wounds he received fighting off the Americans at the Battle of Queenston Heights, on October 13, 1812.

The War of 1812 would forever change the face of Newark and The Harmonious Coach House. In late May of 1813, United States forces captured Fort George and the Newark area. British soldiers were in retreat, except one: Captain Colin Swayze. The folklore says Captain Swayze stopped at The Harmonious Coach House to rendezvous with the innkeeper's daughter, whom he'd fallen in love with. Swayze waited, as American troops closed in, burning buildings and routing out the British. He ran to the cellar of The Coach House and hid in one of the large wooden barrels used to store beer. The American soldiers stormed the building, found Captain Swayze, and killed him in the cellar. Before leaving, the soldiers torched The Coach House.

In 1815, the inn was rebuilt by John Ross and renamed the Sign of the Angel Inn as a loving gesture to Ross's wife. The ghost stories at the Angel Inn began shortly after its reconstruction was complete. According to the inn's owners, in the early 1820s, the ghostly phenomenon made the local newspaper as follows:

> Reports have been received of frequent disturbances during the night at the Sign of the Angel Inn. Local authorities have declined an investigation, pending a formal complaint or the discovery of evidence of wrongdoing.
>
> Upon independent inquiry, this editor has received information of a most unsettling nature, which will raise and terrify the Reader's imagination.
>
> The popular explanation provided by hotel guests and local patrons attributes the nocturnal disturbances to Permutations of the Spirit World. In short, there is a Ghost haunting the Angel Inn.
>
> Footsteps have been heard coming from the darkened dining room, although the source of the sound could not be determined. The clinking of glasses, laughter, and conversation have echoed throughout the Inn, as if emanating from

thin air. Most disturbing was the discovery by the serving staff of table settings, set that previous evening, having been mysteriously arranged.

The Inn's respected proprietor, Mr. Ross, will not dismiss the reports nor contradict the Existence of Apparitions.

The Reader should be mindful of the many unexplained Forces of Nature. There are also those who credit the appearance of Ghosts and Spectres to a tragic past occurrence with an unresolved outcome. Such is the circumstance at the Angel Inn.

There is a popular story of an unfortunate Canadian militia officer who was killed at the Inn during the American invasion of May, 1813.

Captain Colin Swayze had delayed joining the British retreat in order to rendezvous with a young woman, believed to be his true love. Surprised by American soldiers sent to search the Inn, Captain Swayze hid in an empty barrel in the cellar. The invaders used bayonets to prod into every corner and possible place of concealment, and the unlucky lover received a fatal wound.

Some believe the Ghost of Captain Swayze is fated to walk the Inn at night, perhaps in longing for his love. Others suggest the Captain stands sentinel, protecting the property against foreign invaders. It is said that his ghost will remain harmless as long as the British flag flies over the Inn, a precaution prudently taken by the proprietor.

The inn was always a social center for Newark and has been for Niagara-on-the-Lake, as the town was renamed in 1902. At various times in its history, the building served as a library, an apothecary's shop, and as a stop for traveling dentists. It was also a "billet," or military quarters for British officers on colonial duty.

Today the Angel Inn has added "Olde" to its moniker to promote its antiquity, and the building looks much as it did almost two centuries ago, with its hand-cut beams and plank floors that resonate with every step. Inside, Captain Swayze's presence is still felt and experienced as it was just after the rebuilding of the inn. I spoke with Samantha Ling, The Olde Angel Inn's General Manager. The inn has been in Ling's family since March 1992.

Ling described the first paranormal experience that her father, Peter Ling, had during his first night staying at the inn, just before he officially took ownership. Ling said, "One night, when he was here on his own in the building, in the middle of the night, he heard this loud crash and he didn't know what it was. So he ran downstairs and checked all the doors and windows with his flashlight and yelled out silly things like, 'Who's there?' But the building was totally secure, and he couldn't find anything wrong. So he went back upstairs to bed. When he got up in the morning, he went downstairs to the front door to get the newspaper and he discovered his horseshoe, which he had brought over from England, had fallen and been moved about 12 feet from the place where he had put it above the fireplace. That's when he decided that the ghost was welcoming him—hopefully—as the owner of The Angel Inn. And my dad was not a believer in ghosts, per se. So when he told me that, I thought that's definitely a significant story."

Several guests have reported ghostly occurrences over the years that Ling admits are too similar in scope to dismiss. Many guests have claimed to see Captain Swayze at eye-level, while they were in their beds in the inn. Ling said, "They wake up, and he is by their bed—like he's come up through the floor. So he's sort of at eye level with them, and his feet are still below the floor. He appears to them, but as soon as they start to sit up, he disappears."

The staff members have also had their share of encounters. Ling explained how The Olde Angel Inn's bar manager, Graham, was sitting at the bar one night after closing. Graham heard someone walking through the dining room, which is in an adjoining room on the other side of the wall from the bar, so his view was obstructed, and he couldn't see who was producing the footsteps. Graham was worried someone might be trying to break in, so he charged into the dining area only to find the room empty. But curiously, all of the silverware on all of the tables had been scattered.

Laura, who asked me not to use her last name, has worked at The Olde Angel Inn since 1995. She had an encounter in the basement of the building during the winter of 2003. Laura said, "I was closing one night, which I hate doing alone, because it does get a little scary. I was completely locked up, and we had no guests upstairs, so there was no one in the inn at all. And no one else has a key to get in, except for people who live 45 minutes away.

"I went down to do my keg inventory, and then I went into the staff washroom, which is right outside the cellar door. As I was doing my business, somebody started whistling a tune outside the stall. So I did the whole, 'Helloooo… helloooo,' thing. No one. I don't hear anyone walking, and it's an old building so you hear people coming up and down the stairs, especially if there's no one [else] there. I hurried up, opened up the door, but I didn't hear anyone running anywhere; no doors swinging—there just wasn't anyone there."

Laura also mentioned an encounter that happened to one of her friends who works in the kitchen. "She was in the kitchen by herself, and all of a sudden, all the ladles that are hung up in there, they just started swinging, and no one opened a door or anything. There's no wind in the kitchen. She ran out into the wine bar where I was sitting. But there was no one else in there."

Captain Swayze may still hold a grudge to this day. It's been said that kegs of American beer often malfunction at the bar, while the kegs filled with British and Canadian ales work properly. Other strange reports in The Olde Angel Inn include people hearing fife and drum music in one of the bedrooms, spotting apparitions of well-dressed ladies and gentlemen, and occasionally a red-coated man is seen in the reflection in the mirror of the ladies' room.

Ling says some psychics have visited the inn—they tend to show up once or twice a year. One psychic reported no activity at all in the dining room, but when she was taken to the cellar, she became overwhelmed and began to cry. The psychic said there were so many spirits there.

"There's certainly a strong sense of other people in the building when you know there's no one else there," Ling said. "Especially late at night when we're closing the bar, going down to the beer cellar to change kegs, and cleaning up the keg room. A lot of the staff members have heard footsteps only to find nobody there."

Though there may be more than one ghost at The Olde Angel Inn, Captain Swayze is the most prominent. The folklore says the Captain is still looking for his love before he can retreat with his comrades. So long as the Union Jack still flies over the inn, he's content that his hideout is secure.

Chapter 28:
THE WHALEY HOUSE

The Whaley House Museum is open 10 a.m. to 4:30 p.m. every day except Tuesday. After hours, Ghost Tours are available through Ghosts & Gravestones. Contact the museum for more details. Photo by Sande Lollis, Save Our Heritage Organisation.

THE WHALEY HOUSE:

San Diego, California

Tel: 1 (619) 297-9327

Web: *www.whaleyhouse.org*

Imagine getting a good deal on a plot of land in an area that you know is going to grow and prosper. On your land, you build your dream house—but not just a house. In addition to living quarters for your family, this will also serve as your business, with a general store and a giant granary for holding up to 200 tons of grain. Now imagine moving in and finding out it may be haunted. This is Thomas Whaley's story.

Whaley was born into a prominent family, in New York City, on October 5, 1823. His father died when Thomas was only 9 years old, but money was designated for the young boy to get a good education and a jump start in business.

Thomas was ambitious, hardworking, meticulous, and certainly a risk-taker, but luck wasn't on his side in his business ventures. In 1849, a 25-year-old Thomas Whaley left for California, its gold rush, and the prosperity that would surely follow. When Whaley traveled west, he established business contacts and learned about life in California's gold rush. He educated himself about local politics, social circles, and legal matters.

In August of 1852, a man named "Yankee Jim" Robinson and two accomplices were convicted of trying to steal a pilot boat in the harbor called the *Plutus*. Yankee Jim had a reputation of being a ne'er-do-well, and though the two accomplices were sentenced to only a year in prison, Yankee Jim was sentenced to hang by a reportedly intoxicated judge and a jury that included the two owners of the *Plutus*. On September 18, Yankee Jim Robinson, a towering 6-foot 4-inch tall man, was brought to the crude set of gallows in Old Town San Diego, and the hangman's rope was placed around his neck. He was sure this was some stunt to try and scare him, and he continued to make sarcastic comments, even with a rope around his neck. The rope, however, was last used on a much shorter man, and no adjustment was made for the extremely tall Robinson. When the gallows door opened, Robinson's neck didn't snap because the rope was too long. He struggled and slowly strangled to death. The event would quite literally haunt Thomas Whaley, who witnessed the hanging.

In August of 1853, Thomas Whaley went home to New York and married Anna Eloise DeLaunay. The couple returned to San Diego, to grow Whaley's businesses and to start a family. In September of 1855, Whaley found a great deal on some land in Old Town—the very lot where Yankee Jim and many others had met their end at the gallows.

Whaley began building his dream home and storefront in Old Town in September of 1856. The $10,000, two-story, Greek-revival brick mansion—designed and built by Whaley—was the finest structure built in Southern California at the time. The property featured a large, rat-proof brick granary, and the downstairs of the house had plenty of room for Whaley's general store. Inside, the upstairs living quarters featured mahogany and rosewood furniture, Brussels carpets, and damask drapes. But the house had an occupant Whaley hadn't counted on.

The Whaleys had five children and several stores in California over the next 10 years. However, 1858 would be a tough year for the Whaleys. In January, their second-born, Thomas Jr., died at the young age of 18 months. Later that year, an arsonist's flame torched one of Whaley's other businesses located in the Plaza section of Old Town. His grand mansion would be all he had left, but his store there was not doing well.

I spoke with Robin Sweeton, the head docent for the Whaley House since 2002, about some of the early legends the Whaleys experienced shortly after moving in. She said, "He [Whaley] started hearing noises in the house—footsteps upstairs that sounded to him like heavy boot steps. He made comments that he thought Yankee Jim might be haunting his house. That's the legend.... I've heard that it's in his journals."

Whaley rented out part of his house to serve as the county courtroom, and he also rented three rooms upstairs for storage. This brought in $65 per month, which was good income. After citizens of San Diego protested that a more central location would be better suited for the courtroom, the county pulled out of the Whaley House—a deal that soured Whaley, as he felt the county had reneged on their arrangement. The Whaley family became destitute, and Thomas Whaley became a bitter, abusive father and husband.

The next family tragedy to befall the Whaleys happened to their emotionally unstable daughter, Violet Eloise. After a marriage that lasted only two weeks, Violet became suicidal. She had a history of depression, and the failed marriage didn't help her mental state. On August 19, 1885, Violet took her father's pistol to the outside privy and shot herself through the heart. Thomas Whaley carried his daughter into the lounge where she died. The note Violet left read, "Mad from life's history, Swift to death's mystery; Glad to be hurled, Anywhere, anywhere, out of this world."

Thomas Whaley died December 14, 1890, but his widow would live on until February 24, 1913. The Whaley House stayed in the Whaley family until 1953, when Thomas and Anna's daughter, Corinne Lillian died in San Diego and the county assumed ownership of the now dilapidated home.

In 1960, the Whaley House opened as a museum, and the ghost stories got around pretty quickly. I spoke to Dr. Hans Holzer, one of the most notable paranormal investigators in the last century. Holzer has written more than 130 books on the subject and was one of the first to investigate the Whaley House.

Holzer first visited the Whaley House with acclaimed psychic medium Sybil Leek and local television personality and his long-time friend, Regis Philbin. The three encountered the apparition of Anna Whaley. Holzer and Leek were intent on trying to communicate, but this was the first ghost Philbin had ever seen, and he was understandably jumpy. Holzer said, "The older woman, she appeared—it was a very white figure, and Regis got excited and turned on the flashlight, and of course that was the end of the phenomenon. And I keep reminding him of that."

Today, the Save Our Heritage Organisation runs the Whaley House Museum. The docents and volunteers dress in period clothing and are well-versed in the history of the home. They also know the ghost stories, though you'll have to specifically ask to hear them.

Thomas Whaley wouldn't be the last one to hear the lumbering ghostly bootsteps in the house. Sweeton has also heard the strange noises.

She said, "I heard the heavy footsteps upstairs when nobody was there but me. It sounded just like there was somebody else in the house. I heard moving around in a closet and everything, but there was nobody there." Because Whaley was the first to hear them, the heavy footsteps have always been attributed to Yankee Jim.

Sweeton has also smelled perfume and tobacco in the house, when it is quiet and the visitors have all gone for the day. She says, "I pay no attention to anything that might go on, because I attribute it to other people in the house. It's when the house is quiet and there's no air flowing, there's no doors opening and closing, and there's nobody else there when I actually pay attention."

The ghosts haunting the Whaley House are that of Yankee Jim Robinson, Mr. Whaley, his wife Anna, the daughter Violet who committed suicide, and some of the other children who died in the house, including George and Francis, as well as the Whaley's 3-year-old great-granddaughter, visiting from Oceanside, who ingested some ant poison at the home.

Sweeton said, "I think Mr. Whaley just kind of went downhill emotionally. When he died, maybe his daughter was here and he thought, 'Well, I've got to stay here with her and protect her. Or maybe he thought he could fix other problems that he had, that he hadn't been able to resolve during his life, and that might be why he's here. [As for] Mrs. Whaley, I think we keep seeing her running around because she died and they were all there, and she felt like she had to stay too. Like she's there out of the maternal need to remain. If they won't leave, then she feels maybe she has to stay with them."

The ghosts at the Whaley House have been experienced by almost all of the human senses. Witnesses have felt tickled and brushed up against, when there was no one there; apparitions have been seen; perfume and tobacco smelled; and footsteps heard. There's even ghostly music. Sweeton heard a piano after she had closed and locked up for the night. She said, "I had forgotten something and had come right back in. It took me a minute to realize, 'Wait a second, why am I hearing this?' But it was very sweet and happy and a little melodic. As soon as I got my whole self in the door, it just stopped. As if they said, 'Oh, be quiet. She's back.'"

Sweeton's most profound encounter happened one evening, as she was preparing for a ghost tour. She said, "In the master bedroom one evening, at 7:15 p.m., right as a ghost tour was expected at the house, I was upstairs changing my clothes and just getting ready to come downstairs, and I noticed the master bedroom was white inside. I couldn't see in there. I looked in and it was foggy—the whole room was completely foggy. I just stood there kind of transfixed and thought, 'Wow, something's happening. My gosh, I never thought I would see this,' and then I realized I smelled a real heavy, sweet pipe smoke. Then, of course, the doorbell rang and that ruined that experience, and I had to go let people in. By the time I was able to get back up to see it, it was gone and it had dissipated. If it had morphed into a form of any type, I did not get to see that. I may not ever get to see that again in my life. I don't expect to, and I wasn't expecting to when it happened."

Some psychically sensitive guests who have visited the Whaley House have come up to Sweeton after one of her tours and told her that she was not alone in the courtroom and that there was a man standing next to her. When Sweeton asked what he wanted, the psychics seemed to believe he wanted to make sure she got the story right. Some psychics have also said that he doesn't seem to like Sweeton very much. Sweeton said, "As time has gone by and I found out more about this man, not to say he's not a nice person, but the less I like him. I guess if he doesn't like me, it's because I'm not bragging about him and calling him Mr. Wonderful. Apparently he doesn't like that, but I don't care because he has no control."

Sightings of the Whaley House ghosts are reported a few times per year, while hearing things, smelling strange perfumes or tobacco, and other less profound phenomena occur a lot more regularly. Dr. Holzer's theory of why the Whaley House is so haunted is that the people are still strongly tied to the place. He said, "For them, it's still yesterday. There's no sense of time on the other side." For whatever reasons Yankee Jim, Thomas Whaley, and his family have for haunting this historic building, they make their presence known in the Whaley House with regularity. The staff at the Whaley House believe the Whaleys may be a bit put-off by the fact that so many people come through their home each day. If you stop in for a visit, be sure to wipe your feet and take off your hat before entering—you're a guest of the Whaley's here. And if they don't like you, they may find a way to show it.

Chapter 29:
THE TOWER OF LONDON

The Tower of London offers tours seven days a week. Check with the Tower for prices and times. They recommend planning on 2 to 3 hours for your visit. Photo by Roberto Aberasturia.

THE TOWER OF LONDON:

London, England

Tel: 44 (0) 870-756-6060

Web: *www.hrp.org.uk*

TOP SECRET

The Tower of London is built of stone and mortar, its walkways are paved with brick and rock, but below your feet, and below the rock, countless pints of blood have seeped, spilled from some of the many historically notable prisoners who spent their final days within the Tower's walls.

Ghost sightings at the Tower have been happening since the mid-13th century, and many of these spirits are pure royalty. The ghosts of princes, queens, countesses, children, and many others have been seen, felt, or heard over the centuries by the Tower's Yeoman Warders and its visitors.

The Tower's earliest, central structure was built by William the Conqueror of Normandy, between 1066 and 1067 c.e. King William I chose the site along the shores of the River Thames and built the initial structure into the southeast corner of the Roman city walls. By the late 1070s, the White Tower was completed by Norman masons and Anglo-Saxon laborers. It was the tallest building in London for many centuries. This fortress has served vitally important roles to Britain ever since, including a royal palace, an armory, a prison, the central stage of executions in London, a mint, and home to the Crown Jewels.

Over the next 480 years, expansion projects by various kings would include building curtain walls featuring towers with names such as Byward, Beauchamp, Devereux, Bloody, Salt, Lanthorn, Martin, Flint, and several more. A great moat around three sides of the complex connected to the Thames, and a wharf separated the moat from the river. Inside the walls of the fortress, barracks, stables, the Jewel House, and a formal housing facility called the Queen's House were built. With each century, the Tower of London became an increasingly formidable and awesome fortress. Today, when you talk about the Tower of London, you're actually talking about more than 20 towers, as well as many buildings inside the stronghold walls.

When a visitor steps into the Tower of London today, they step into a millennia of British history. The dark, foreboding castle walls rise around each visitor, and if you combine the setting with London's autumn fog off the Thames or a light mist of rain, you're bound to get a chill from a place that is considered by many to be the most haunted on Earth.

For an insider's view of what life, death, and ghosts in the Tower of London are like, I spoke with Yeoman Sergeant Phil Wilson, a Yeoman Warder and full-time resident of the Tower since 1996. Wilson is also the resident expert on the ghost legends.

To become a Yeoman Warder at the Tower of London, one must have served in the armed forces for at least 22 years, reached the rank of staff sergeant or higher, be a recipient of the Long Service and Good Conduct medal, and have a character reference of "exemplary" when they leave the service. After that, an interview process determines who will make the cut into this elite group. There are currently 35 Yeoman Warders in the world, and these Warders have overseen the Tower of London for many centuries. The Beefeaters, as they came to be called informally, started as bodyguards for King Henry VIII, in 1485, and they can be spotted in their scarlet and gold dress uniforms or their more dressed-down scarlet and blue uniforms. Wilson and his wife have lived in Beauchamp Tower since they first moved into the Tower of London, and though Wilson doesn't consider himself a believer in ghosts yet, he is very well-versed in the ghostly legends of the Tower, and he has had a few unexplained personal experiences himself.

Yeoman Warder Wilson first came to the Tower when he served guard duty in 1967. He said, "In 1967, the Tower was a very different place. There weren't the lights around the area; it was quite a scary place." Before serving guard duty, and before military service, Wilson heard about the ghost stories in the Tower of London when he was a child. He heard about the story of Queen Anne Boleyn from the 1935 song, "Anne Boleyn," by R.P. Weston and Bert Lee. The chorus of the song goes,

"With her head tucked underneath her arm / She walks the Bloody Tower! With her head tucked underneath her arm / At the Midnight hour."

Anne Boleyn was the second of King Henry VIII's six wives, and they were married in 1533. Henry VIII plotted against his wife and had her investigated for infidelity and treason. She was found guilty and executed at the Tower of London on May 19, 1536. She is one of the most persistent ghostly figures seen there, according to literature published by the Tower.

The headless female figure of Anne Boleyn is occasionally spotted drifting from the Queen's House within the Tower walls, across to the Chapel of St. Peter ad Vincula. She's said to lead a procession of dignitaries down the aisle to her final resting place under the altar.

One of the more gruesome haunts is that of Margaret Plantagenet, the Countess of Salisbury. Henry VIII didn't agree with Margaret's staunch Roman Catholic beliefs and viewed her as a political threat. She was 68 years old when Henry VIII ordered her head to be placed on the chopping block at Tower Green. On May 27, 1541, the Countess of Salisbury refused to put her head on the block like a common traitor, and ran from the executioner who hacked her to death with his axe. Witnesses have seen the act replay itself in the Green, and others have seen the shadow of the axe fall on the nearby stone wall.

On July 17, 1674, some workers were dismantling the staircase of the White Tower for a reconstruction project, when they discovered two small skeletons. In Alison Weir's book, *The Princes in the Tower*, she says, "It was immediately assumed that these were the bodies of the Princes in the Tower. An anonymous eyewitness wrote: 'This day I, standing by the opening, saw working men dig out of a stairway in the White Tower the bones of those two Princes who were foully murdered by Richard III. They were small bones of lads in their teens, and there were pieces of rag and velvet about them.' They were, he adds, 'fully recognized to be the bones of those two Princes.'"

The two Princes were 12-year-old King Edward V and his 9-year-old brother, Richard, Duke of York. The two boys were murdered under suspicious circumstances in 1483. One story says it was Richard III who plotted the murder, while others say it was Henry Tudor (who would become King Henry VII) who ordered the deed done. Regardless, the elder boy was stabbed to death while his brother was suffocated with a pillow. Their bodies were hidden—buried near the foundation of the White Tower.

The Princes have been spotted in the Bloody Tower wearing white nightgowns and holding hands. They never make a sound and can only be seen for a few fleeting moments before they fade into the stonework.

As a Yeoman Warder and tour guide for the Tower, Wilson gets asked about the ghosts a lot, especially by the children, who are eager to frighten their siblings. Wilson tells the children that, with one exception, none of the ghosts has ever killed anybody.

That one exception happened in January of 1815, at the stroke of midnight, to a sentry who was patrolling in the Martin Tower. The sentry saw a cloud of smoke slide in from under the doorway. The mist took the form of a giant, gray bear. The sentry lunged at the bear with his bayonet, but passed right through—his bayonet stuck in the door. It took two soldiers to pull the blade free. The sentry told his comrades what had transpired and died of fright two days later.

Wilson told me about the story a retired Yeoman Warder told him. Wilson said, "He told me that he lived in one of the quarters around the casements, which are in the outer circle of the Tower. His story goes that he was fast asleep one night, no problems at all, and then he was shaken awake by his wife, who said, 'Who were those two children standing at the end of the bed in white nightgowns?' Of course he woke up and had seen absolutely nothing, She then went on to describe these two children as looking quite distressed, and they were in long, white nightgowns cuddling each other in front of a Victorian fireplace. Of course, there was no Victorian fireplace there at all. So you put it down to a dream or whatever. Anyway, they [the couple] moved from the quarters to somewhere else, and they started redecorating the quarter and found there was actually a false wall behind which was a Victorian fireplace. So that gave that story a bit more credence."

Yeoman Warder Wilson's own unexplained encounter happened to him in his living quarters in the Beauchamp Tower. He said, "I'm one of these people that likes music wherever I go, and I would take a radio into the shower room, and occasionally the radio would actually throw itself off the windowsill for no apparent reason whatsoever. I, of course, not particularly believing in ghosts, although I talk a lot about them, put it down to some sort of subsidence [settling of the building], but you never know. And quite often we've come home and found all the towels in the bathroom piled in the middle of the floor. My wife swears it's me, but I can honestly say it isn't."

With so many famous executions at the Tower, some of the historically obscure ghosts also seem to want recognition. Wilson described a discovery in a lower chamber of the Beauchamp Tower in 2001. The Beauchamp Tower specifically was used extensively as a state prison. These prisoners left their mark in the form of engravings all over the prison walls. Wilson said, "This lady came with her daughter early one morning and was talking to the Yeoman Warder. The daughter started to go into sort of a semi-trance and said, 'So much suffering...' When the Yeoman Warder asked if she was all right, the mother said, 'Oh, yes. She gets the vibes'—we come across it a lot at the Tower. He then went on and said the lady was quite interested in the engravings. There's one engraving in a small back room, which is actually a crucifix that's been engraved in the wall, and obviously someone used this as an altar during the time they were prisoner there. During this conversation, the girl started again with 'So much suffering...' to which the Yeoman Warder replied, 'Oh yes, but they've all gone now.' The young lady, without turning around, put her hand behind her back as if to put it on somebody's shoulder who sat at the window, and said, 'This man is still here.' To which the Yeoman Warder said, 'Oh, well who's that?' And again, without looking at the wall, she put her hand straight on the inscription: 'Thomas Talbert 1496.' That engraving is not in any of the Tower publications, the room is not open to the pubiic, so I can't see how she'd have had any previous knowledge of where the engraving was. Of course, at that point, the Yeoman Warder ushered them out, and off they went."

The girl's blind identification of that particular name, among the dozens on the wall, of a man with no known historical significance, demonstrates that even the unknown spirits have a story to tell. Wilson claims that, since Thomas Talbert's name has been discovered, his radio no longer flies off the windowsill and the towels no longer get piled into the middle of his floor. He said, "It was some six or seven months later that a different lady came, [who was] previously in the same tower, same chamber, and inquired of the Yeoman Warder on duty if there were any changes been made to this room. The Yeoman Warder said, 'Well, apart from the odd coat of paint, nothing really.' To which she said, 'Well I was here 30 years ago, and this room was very foreboding. It's now actually quite comforting.'"

For Halloween 2001, Ross Hemsworth, Managing Director for Galaxi Television, took his "Phantom or Fraud" project to the Tower of London for a live Webcast and television special on the ghosts there. Hemsworth told me about his brush with the unexplained at the Tower. "It was quite strange, actually, because we're quite a scientific research organization, so we tend to be fairly logical and rational in the way we go about our work," he said. "But we had some of the best evidence supporting the orb theory while we were at the Tower of London, because in the past, most of us have put the orbs down to either dust or moisture in the air—airborne particles that are photographed out of focus on digital cameras and video. However, on this particular occasion, our still photographer at the time, Graham Matthews—who was a total skeptic—was photographing his brother on the steps to the Bloody Tower. And he basically said to Andy that he felt as if something had just gone right through him. Andy at that point had said, 'Yes, it's a little girl. She's standing right in front of me.' Andy Matthews is one of our presenters, but he's also a clairvoyant. His eyes were looking down at the front of his chest, and when the photograph was taken, there's a glowing orb on Andy's chest. So it's the first time we've been able to actually measure depth of field on one of these things. Andy asked it to move and return to the bottom of the stairs, and it was next photographed at the bottom of the stairs, thus indicating an intelligence, which again would rule out dust, pollen, moisture, et cetera. So there was some good evidence, and there were several occasions over the two nights where we had very similar things happen with Andy and with other members of the team. It is supposed to be the most haunted [place] in the world, and we've got evidence there to support that particular theory."

The Byward Tower is where the guards sit to watch the main gate. After hours, it's their job to unlock the door for the Tower's residents, who may be returning after its been locked for the evening. Wilson told of a retired Yeoman Warder who recounted his own experience in the Byward Tower around 1998. Wilson said, "There was one Yeoman Warder who was on duty there at 1:00 or 2:00 in the morning, who sat reading the paper, and he had a gas fire running. You know how you get a hiss from a gas fire? He claims that the room went slightly darker, and the hiss changed to a crackling, as if it was a log fire. He turned to the great Norman fireplace, and sure enough, the gas fire had gone and there was a log fire burning. Standing on each side of the log fire was what he only could describe as two very thin men with spindly legs, dressed in red, smoking long, white clay pipes. He claims that he looked at them, one of the—for want of a better word—Yeoman Warders looked back at him, and when they made eye contact, they vanished. That's one story that has really taken. One or two people don't like doing duty in there on their own to this day."

It has been said that the Yeoman Warders don't like to speak of the ghosts, for fear of stirring them up. However, Yeoman Wilson says, "It certainly doesn't worry me. When you first come to the Tower, it's quite awe-inspiring to be sleeping in a place that's over 1,000 years old. The first time I came back to the Tower alone, late at night, I was walking through the Tower, and the hairs on the back of your neck do tend to stand on end.

"If there are going to be ghosts anywhere, they've got to be at the Tower of London."

Afterword

Your haunted world tour doesn't have to end when you close this book! Ghostvillage.com is the largest supernatural community on the Web. Since Jeff Belanger launched the site in 1999, Ghostvillage.com has been home to ghost research, evidence, and discussion from around the world. The Website features a giant library of personal ghost encounters from famous, infamous, and completely obscure locales. Thousands of people visit the community forums—people who are ghost hunters, researchers, or in some cases, victims of a haunting. On the site, you'll find ghost photos, audio recordings, and even videos, as well as Jeff Belanger's online column, "Legends of the Supernatural."

Additionally, there is an entire section of the Website devoted to this book. You'll find further resources on each chapter, and there will be an opportunity for other witnesses of supernatural phenomena to submit their own experiences from each location covered in *The World's Most Haunted Places*. We hope to see you online for even more haunted places at *www.ghostvillage.com/wmhp*.

Resources

BBCi. "Ghost Watch—The Ballygally Ghost Room." 24 Feb 2004. *<www.bbc.co.uk/northernireland/autumn/halloween/ghost1.shtml>*.

BBCi. "Tom Foolery and Muncaster Castle." 10 Mar 2004. *<www.bbc.co.uk/cumbria/features/askaway/people/ tom_fool.shtml>*.

Bell, Michael E. *Food for the Dead: On the Trail of New England's Vampires.* New York: Carroll & Graf Publishers, 2001.

Bergan, Dan. "The Hibbing High School." (Historical brochure published by the high school) Hibbing, Minnesota, 2001.

De Lisser, Herbert G. *The White Witch of Rose Hall.* Kingston, Jamaica: Macmillan Caribbean, 1958.

Fancher, Betsy. *Savannah: A Renaissance of the Heart.* Garden City, N.Y.: Doubleday & Company, Inc., 1976.

Ferrell, Nancy Warren. "The Founding of Juneau, Alaska." 6 Nov 2003. *<www.juneau.lib.ak.us/community/history/junohist.htm>*.

Fry, Plantagenet Somerset. *Castles of Britain and Ireland.* New York: Abbeville Press, 1997.

Garcez, Antonio R. *Adobe Angels: Arizona Ghost Stories.* Santa Fe, N.Mex.: Red Rabbit Press, 1998.

Garrett, Wendell, ed. *Our Changing White House.* Boston: Northeastern University Press, 1995.

Hauck, Dennis William. *Haunted Places: The National Directory.* New York: Penguin Books, 1996.

———. *The International Directory of Haunted Place.* New York: Penguin Books, 2000.

Heller, Herbert L., ed. *Sourdough Sagas.* Cleveland and New York: The World Publishing Company, 1967.

Henderson, Robert. "The Capture of Fort George, May 2th, 1813." 23 Mar 2004. *<www.warof1812.ca/ftgeorge.htm>*.

Holzer, Hans. *True Ghost Stories.* New York: Dorset Press, 2001.

Inpey, Edward, and Geoffrey Parnell. *The Tower of London: The Official Illustrated History*. London: Merrell Publishers, 2000.

Kenyon, John. *The Popish Plot*. London: Phoenix Press, 1972.

Lincoln Institute, The. "William Wallace Lincoln (1850-1862)." 20 Jan 2004. *<http://www.mrlincolnswhitehouse.org/templates/ display.search.cfm?ID=18>*.

Miller, William H., and David F. Hutchings. *Transatlantic Liners at War: The Story of the Queens*. New York: Arco Publishing, 1985.

Myers, Arthur. *The Ghostly Register: Haunted Dwellings, Active Spirits*. Chicago: Contemporary Books, 1986.

Rule, Leslie. *Coast to Coast Ghosts*. Kansas City, Mo.: Andrews McMeel Publishing, 2001.

Smith, Barbara. *Ghost Stories from Alberta*. Willowdale, Ontario: Hounslow Press, 1993.

Sterry, Iveagh, and William Garrigus. *They Found a Way*. Brattleboro, Vt.: Daye Press, 1938.

Stevenson, Robert Louis. *Treasure Island*. New York: Signet, 1998.

Vallois, Thirza. *Around and About Paris, Volume 1*. London: Iliad Books, 1995.

Wendt, Ron. *Haunted Alaska: Ghost Stories from the Far North*. Kenmore, Wash.: Epicenter Press, 2002.

Wilson, Alan J., Des Brogan, and Frances Hollinrake. *Hidden & Haunted: Underground Edinburgh*. Edinburgh, Scotland: Mercat Tours of Edinburgh, 1999.

Index

About the Author

Jeff Belanger is a voracious fan of the unexplained. He's been studying and writing about the supernatural for regional and national publications since 1997. In 1999, Belanger launched Ghostvillage.com as a repository for his writings. Since then, the site has grown to become the largest paranormal community on the Web, attracting hundreds of thousands of visitors per year. He currently haunts Bellingham, Massachusetts, with his wife, Megan.